Shamanic Plant Medicine

Magic Mushrooms: The Holy Children

Shamanic Plant Medicine

Magic Mushrooms: The Holy Children

Ross Heaven

Winchester, UK
Washington, USA

First published by Moon Books, 2019
Moon Books is an imprint of John Hunt Publishing Ltd., No. 3 East Street, Alresford
Hampshire SO24 9EE, UK
office1@jhpbooks.net
www.johnhuntpublishing.com
www.moon-books.net

For distributor details and how to order please visit the 'Ordering' section on our website.

ISBN: 978 1 78279 251 2
978 1 78279 250 5 (ebook)
Library of Congress Control Number: 2018930207

A CIP catalogue record for this book is available from the British Library.

Design: Stuart Davies

UK: Printed and bound by CPI Group (UK) Ltd, Croydon, CR0 4YY
US: Printed and bound by Thomson Shore, 7300 West Joy Road, Dexter, MI 48130

Contents

About the Author

Ross Heaven was a shaman and the author of several books on shamanism, plant teachers and healing. He ran ceremonies and workshops on these themes in Europe and Peru, including Shamanic Apprenticeship training programmes, Shamanic Healing and Soul Retrieval courses, as well as plant medicine retreats with San Pedro, Salvia divinorum, mushrooms and ayahuasca.

There is a website at www.thefourgates.org where you can read more about his work as well as his books and other items of interest.

For Katya Sinyukova, the mother of the children, and Bodge, who was there for the most magical adventure of Mexico.

Introduction

Shamanic Plant Medicine: The First Practical Guides to Working with Teacher Plants

Shamanic Plant Medicine is a series of books written to provide you with a succinct and practical introduction to a specific teacher or power plant, its history, shamanic uses, healing applications and benefits, as well as the things to be aware of when working with these plants, including ceremonial procedures and safety precautions. These plants are also known in the Western world as entheogens: substances which "reveal the God within," and in shamanic cultures as allies: helpful spirits which confer power and pass on insights and information.

The first in this series are *Ayahuasca: The Vine of Souls, San Pedro: The Gateway to Wisdom, Salvia Divinorum: The Sage of the Seers* and *Magic Mushrooms: The Holy Children*. It is a series which reveals the truth about these plants and provides an insight into their uses as well as the cautions to take with them so you are properly informed of your choices not reliant on government propaganda, media sensationalism and disinformation. Then you can make your own decisions.

The shamanic use of plants and herbs is one of the world's oldest healing methods and, despite government and media campaigns to the contrary it is usually the safest and most effective form of medicine too. In 2005, for example, the *British Medical Journal* warned that "in England alone reactions to [legally available prescription] drugs that led to hospitalisation followed by death are estimated at 5,700 a year and could actually be closer to 10,000." By comparison, in the *four* years between 2000 and August 2004 there were just 451 reports of adverse reactions to herbal preparations and only 152 were considered serious.

No fatalities. That statistic equates to just 38 problem cases a year resulting from plant medicines compared to perhaps 10,000 deaths a year as a result of accepted mainstream medicine. Reviewing these figures the London *Independent* newspaper concluded that "Herbs may not be completely safe as critics like to point out – but they are a lot safer than drugs."

The situation in America is similar. Here, orthodox medical treatment itself is now the leading cause of death, ahead of heart disease and cancer, and "Infections, surgical mistakes and other medical harm contributes to the deaths of 180,000 hospital patients a year [and] another 1.4 million are seriously hurt by their hospital care" (Consumer Reports online: www.consumerreports.org). Even more sobering is the fact revealed by other studies that adverse drug reactions are under-reported by up to 94 percent in the US since the government does not adequately track them. Deaths as a result of plant healings meanwhile remain next to zero, and they can be as effective – or more so – than prescription medications.

It is worth asking why these figures so often go unreported and why the medical profession continues to treat people as it does even with full awareness of the risks and comparisons. Another good question is why plants and herbs more than drugs and orthodox medicine are the focus of governments for stricter regulation (see for example the current *codex alimentarius* proposals) despite their effectiveness and comparative freedom from risk. Who benefits, especially financially, from this state of affairs?

More remarkable even than their ability to heal the body is the ability of some plants to expand the mind, raise consciousness, release stuck or damaging emotions and connect us more deeply to spirit. These are the teacher plants. By showing us our true power and potential they enable us to see through illusions and explore the real nature of the universe so we discover our purpose on Earth.

Plant teachers are used by shamans the world over in a sacred ritual context to divine the future, enter spirit realms, learn the deepest truths of themselves and the universe (although many shamans see little distinction between the two since, as they say, "the world is as you dream it," that is, each of us *is* the universe). They also enable them – and us – to perform true healings which go beyond the abilities of modern medicine and its reliance on intrusive treatments and often damaging drugs.

Magic Mushrooms: The Holy Children

Long before trees overtook the land, Earth was covered by giant mushrooms. 24 feet tall and three feet wide, these giant spires dotted the ancient landscape ... From around 420 to 350 million years ago, when land plants were still the relatively new kids on the evolutionary block and "the tallest trees stood just a few feet high" giant spires of life poked from the Earth.
Smithsonian Institute article[1]

When we bear in mind the beatific sense of awe and ecstasy and caritas engendered by the divine mushrooms, one is emboldened to the point of asking whether they may not have planted in primitive man the very idea of god.
Robert Gordon Wasson, ethnomycologist

There is a world beyond ours, a world that is far away, nearby, and invisible, and that is where God lives, where the dead live, the spirits and the saints. A world where everything has already happened and everything is known. That world talks. It has a language of its own. I report what it says. The sacred mushroom takes me by the hand and brings me to the world where everything is known. It is they, the sacred mushrooms that speak in a way that I can understand. I ask them and they answer me. When I return from the trip that I have taken with them, I tell what they have told me and what they have shown me.
Maria Sabina, mushroom shaman

1

The Sainted Ones and the "Mushroom Meme-Men"

Whether the mushrooms came from outer space or not, the presence of psychedelic substances in the diet of early human beings created a number of changes in our evolutionary situation.
Terence McKenna, "charismatic talking head"

The relationship between human beings and magic mushrooms (known in Mexico as "the sainted ones" or "the holy children") is, supposedly, an ancient one. Gordon Wasson, the ethnobotanist, for example, dribbling his enthusiasm everywhere like the spores of the fungi he so admired, gushed that they may "have planted in primitive man the very idea of god." Other enthusiasts point to rock paintings from Tassili in North Africa which allegedly depict a human-like creature which they believe to be a mushroom shaman in communion with the spirit of his teacher plant sprouting mushrooms from his body and arms.[2] You can Google tassili+mushroom+man to view the images. The fact that these paintings date from the Mesolithic period – up to 22,000 years ago (between 20,000-10,000 BCE) – shows the antiquity of our relationship with these plants, the mushroom enthusiasts say.

Furthermore, "mushroom stones" dating from 200 CE have been found in Guatemala, demonstrating an ancient reverence for sacred mushrooms, while *teonanácatl* (literally "divine mushroom")[3] were served at the coronation of the Aztec ruler Moctezuma II in 1502. Together these instances, recorded in art and history, show a continuity of mushroom use across thousands of years; again, in the opinion of mushroom enthusiasts.

The first mention of psychedelic mushroom taking in Europe,

meanwhile, appeared in the *London Medical and Physical Journal* in 1799, in a story which recounted how a man accidentally served his family "magic" *(psilocybin)* mushrooms for breakfast after picking them in a local park. Upon receiving medical assistance the family appeared confused but not overly-distressed and the attending doctor noted that the youngest child "was attacked with fits of immoderate laughter, nor could the threats of his father or mother refrain him."[4]

The reason for our long-standing relationship with mushrooms is natural and obvious according to people like Terence McKenna, who spent a lot of his time dabbling with them last century: early man, foraging for food, would simply have come across them by accident, ate them, tripped out, liked it and repeated until enlightenment. There's a bit more to this –his "stoned monkey" theory – as we'll see later, but actually not much more.

As Andy Letcher warns us in his book *Shroom,* however,

> ...whenever anything is deemed "natural" and "obvious" it almost always turns out, on closer inspection, to be culturally specific, localised and historically contingent – in other words, not at all natural or obvious ... The belief in the ancientness of psychedelia is no exception for it turns out, somewhat paradoxically, to have rather recent origins,

Not prehistoric at all in fact but "a product of the utopian sentiments that accompanied the psychedelic revolution of the 1950s and 1960s."

Such "utopian sentiments" may have led some of the people who were part of this revolution to see mushrooms everywhere and exaggerate the evidence for their usage. One example is the Tassili cave painting itself (again, Google tassili+mushroom+man to see the images), a piece of trippy historical art which is often presented as "proof" of our ancient involvement with mushrooms.

The classic image you see in books and online though, all crisp and clear and obviously mushroom-ic, is not the one which appears on the wall of the cave. It is, instead, a cleaned-up pen-and-ink drawing based loosely on the original which was made by Terence McKenna's wife, Kat Harrison (a mushroom enthusiast herself and hardly an objective witness) to prove a point about the antiquity of mushroom usage, so not exactly a scientific study since she more-or-less ignored the data and cheated.

Even without this cheat, however, the image itself is ambiguous. The cleaned-up version apparently shows mushrooms growing from the body and arms of the shaman it represents, but if you're not looking for mushrooms in the first place these objects could just as easily be arrows or spades, body armor or hair. And maybe he's not a shaman but a hunter, a gardener, a warrior or ... wait for it ... a bee. I mean, why do we suppose he's even human? He looks more like a bee than a mushroom in Harrison's drawing, after all – which is another mystery since bees have nothing to do with mushrooms in either the botanical or the shamanic world (although mushrooms store well in honey and they can also be taken that way). In short, this image is really not *proof* of anything except wishful thinking by hippies.

But even if all the evidence stacked up and we could trace a neat line back through history to show mankind's uninterrupted use of mushrooms, there would still be no reason to believe that this was deliberate, purposeful or had any shamanic intention. As Letcher points out,

> In Europe ... psilocybin mushrooms have been known about since at least as long ago as the fifteenth century ... but no-one seems to have eaten them intentionally until the twentieth ... [In fact] It seems that everywhere we look in the dim and distant past, those slippery and evanescent mushrooms

> simply evade our grasp. There are none to be found in the archeological record ... Supposed images of mushrooms are, in the absence of contextual information, quite possibly something else entirely, while purported hallucinogenically inspired rock art may be nothing of the sort. Not one single line of evidence unequivocally points to their having been used by Druids, herbalists, Stone Age architects or prehistoric shamans ... [if our distant ancestors were indeed mushroom stoners] they left not a single piece of evidence.

He concludes that "while people appear to have been eating hallucinogenic mushrooms for as long as there have been records, until the twentieth century they always did so accidentally and unintentionally."

Well, that sucks

Yes, I know. We have been conditioned to believe in the ancient use of sacred mushrooms but, as Oscar Wilde wrote, "The truth is rarely pure and never simple." I'm coming clean now about our cozy and taken-for-granted "known certainties" of archaic shamanic mushroom use so we can start learning about what mushrooms really are and do instead of accepting without question everything that they're not. In fact, most of our knowledge (or at least what we think of as knowledge but is more often disinformation) about shrooms in the modern world comes from the work of three individuals, none of whom is an entirely reliable witness:

- R. (Robert) Gordon Wasson, one of the first Westerners to participate in an indigenous Mazatec mushroom ceremony, in Huautla de Jimenez, near Oaxaca, Mexico, with the then-unknown and now infamous *curandera* (shaman) Maria Sabina.
- Timothy Leary, a Harvard psychologist who was inspired

by Wasson's mushroom adventures and traveled to Mexico to experience them for himself in a non-ceremonial setting (at a pool party with friends). His life was changed by what he discovered and he returned to America to begin the Harvard Psilocybin Project, a controversial enterprise which eventually got him sacked from Harvard and led to a new career as "the most dangerous man in America." As the "turn on, tune in, drop out" countercultural leader, hippie spokesperson, and "drugs guru" of the 1960s, he became the mushroom man of his time.

- Terence McKenna, an ethnobotanist and self-styled "psychonaut" who, with his brother Dennis, undertook "the experiment at La Chorrera," a bizarre encounter with *cubensis* mushrooms in the Amazon jungle which led to a series of even stranger noodlings about human evolution and destiny and to philosophical ponderings from both brothers for many years to come about the nature of reality and the role of mushrooms in our ancient past and possible futures.

These three men have entered public consciousness to the extent that they have become the "meme-men" for mushrooms and it is their words (especially Terence McKenna's) you will most often see staring back at you from the Facebook page of a "true believer," accompanied by rainbow-colored spaced-out trippy visuals. We have been left, sadly, with the two or three-sentence soundbites of these men (often the more bizarre or platitudinous the better) as the summation of our modern consumer knowledge of, and "buyer's guide" to, magic mushrooms, yet they actually tell us next-to-nothing about mushrooms, shamanism, healing, or the ceremonial experience but are rather the vacuous slogans of trip-heads aimed at airheads. Before we move on to look at mushroom use in a true shamanic context, therefore, it is worth exploring what these three individuals have to say to see what (if any) of it may be useful to us in our more than veneer-deep engagements with the sacred through the agency of the "wondrous mushroom."

R. Gordon Wasson and His Betrayal of Maria Sabina

Robert Gordon Wasson (1898–1986) journeyed to Huautla, Mexico, with his friend Allan Richardson (and later, his wife, Valentina) to study the religious use of mushrooms as part of the research for his book, *Mushrooms, Russia and History* (published in 1957). During this trip, according to the not so self-effacing Wasson, "Richardson and I [became] the first white men in recorded history to eat the divine mushrooms" in a Mazatec *velada* (night-time candle-lit ceremonial healing vigil) "which for centuries [had] been a secret of certain Indian peoples living far from the great world in southern Mexico. No anthropologists had ever described the scene that we witnessed."

The ceremony was led by the *curandera* (female shaman/ healer) Maria Sabina, who welcomed Wasson to the event and also allowed him to take her picture on the condition that he kept it private, a courtesy which Wasson returned by breaking his promise to her almost immediately and publishing not only the photo but her name and that of the community she served in his book; a betrayal that would come to have wide-ranging and long-lasting negative consequences, as we shall see.

In May 1957 Wasson described his ceremonial experience in an article for *Life* magazine, entitled *Seeking the Magic Mushroom* (subtitle: *Great adventures in the discovery of mushrooms that cause strange visions* – which sounds very Boy's Own Adventure-ish and gives us another glimpse into Wasson's character).[5] This time he kept his promise to Sabina that he would protect her anonymity (although by then the damage was already done) and referred to her in his writing as "Eva Mendez ... a curandera *de primera categoría*, of the highest quality, *una Señora sin mancha*, a woman without stain."

He depicted the ceremony, and his feelings during it, as follows:

> At about 10:30 o'clock Eva Mendez cleaned the mushrooms of their grosser dirt and then, with prayers, passed them through the smoke of resin incense burning on the floor [probably copal]. As she did this, she sat on a mat before a simple altar table adorned with Christian images, the Child Jesus and the Baptism in Jordan. Then she apportioned the mushrooms among the adults. She reserved 13 pair for herself and 13 pair for her daughter. (The mushrooms are always counted in pairs.) I was on tiptoe of expectancy: she turned and gave me six pair in a cup. I could not have been happier: this was the culmination of years of pursuit. She gave Allan six pair too … Then we ate our mushrooms, chewing them slowly, over the course of a half hour. They tasted bad – acrid with a rancid odour that repeated itself[6]…

Actually, this is hardly, if ever, true. Mushrooms taste "earthy" (especially if freshly picked), as you would expect; maybe a little "cardboardy," certainly not "bad", and their taste (if any) is fleeting. It does not "repeat." Their smell, if fresh, might also best be described as earthy while, if dry, they have next to no aroma. In either case, "rancid" is an inappropriate term.

Before midnight, he goes on, 'Eva Mendez' broke a flower from the bouquet on her altar and used it to snuff out the flame of the room's only candle, leaving the group in silent darkness before she began an invocation to the spirits in the name of Christ and the saints, and the mushrooms took effect.

> For the first time the word ecstasy took on real meaning. For the first time it did not mean someone else's state of mind … The visions had started. They reached a plateau of intensity

> deep in the night, and they continued at that level until about 4 o'clock ... the visions came whether our eyes were opened or closed. They emerged from the center of the field of vision, opening up as they came, now rushing, now slowly, at the pace that our will chose. They were in vivid color, always harmonious. They began with art motifs, angular such as might decorate carpets or textiles or wallpaper or the drawing board of an architect. Then they evolved into palaces with courts, arcades, gardens – resplendent palaces all laid over with semiprecious stones. Then I saw a mythological beast drawing a regal chariot. Later it was as though the walls of our house had dissolved and my spirit had flown forth, and I was suspended in mid-air viewing landscapes of mountains with camel caravans advancing slowly across the slopes, the mountains rising tier above tier to the very heavens ... The visions were not blurred or uncertain. They were sharply focused, the lines and colors being so sharp that they seemed more real to me than anything I had ever seen with my own eyes. I felt that I was now seeing plain, whereas ordinary vision gives us an imperfect view; I was seeing the archetypes, the Platonic ideas that underlie the imperfect images of everyday life ... the effect of the mushrooms is to bring about a fission of the spirit, a split in the person, a kind of schizophrenia, with the rational side continuing to reason and to observe the sensations that the other side is enjoying..

"Mendez" accompanied the visions with a low humming which became syllables, then words and then "a full-bodied canticle, sung like very ancient music", which would rise to a climax and then suddenly stop before the curandera returned to "hot, crisp words that cut the darkness like a knife", which Wasson interpreted as "God's words" – the mushroom spirit speaking through her like an oracle, answering problems that had been posed by her participants.

Wasson was clearly excited by his experience. "For a day following our mushroom adventure [sic] Allan and I did little but discuss [it]", he tells us.

> We had attended a shamanistic rite with singing and dancing among our Mixeteco friends which no anthropologist has ever before described in the New World, a performance with striking parallels in the shamanistic practices of some of the archaic Palaeo-Siberian peoples. But may not the meaning of what we had witnessed go beyond this?...
>
> In man's evolutionary past, as he groped his way out from his lowly past, there must have come a moment in time when he discovered the secret of the hallucinatory mushrooms. Their effect on him, as I see it, could only have been profound, a detonator to new ideas. For the mushrooms revealed to him worlds beyond the horizons known to him, in space and time, even worlds on a different plane of being, a heaven and perhaps a hell. For the credulous primitive mind, the mushrooms must have reinforced mightily the idea of the miraculous ...
>
> When we bear in mind the beatific sense of awe and ecstasy and caritas engendered by the divine mushrooms, one is emboldened to the point of asking whether they may not have planted in primitive man the very idea of god ... It is no accident, perhaps, that the first answer of the Spanishspeaking Indian, when I asked about the effect of the mushrooms, was often this: *Le llevan ahí donde Dios está*, "They carry you there where God is"...

According to Wasson (although where he got this information is not clear), magic mushrooms are not used as "therapeutic agents: they themselves do not effect cures" but tell the curandera how to act, what to say or what advice to give in order to create a cure. They may also be consulted directly or via the shaman if participants are "distraught with grave problems" such as the theft of a donkey (sic) so they can learn where it is and who took it, or to find out how a relative in another town or country is faring, in which case the mushrooms act like "a kind of a postal service".

Mushrooms are non-addictive, he tells us. "When the rainy season is over and the mushrooms disappear, there seems to be no physiological craving for them", nor does dosage increase with use, although "Some persons require more than others. ["An increase in the dose intensifies the experience but does not greatly prolong the effect"]". Prolonged usage, even with large doses, causes no harm. "We think the mushrooms have no cumulative effect on the human organism. Eva Mendez has been taking them for 35 years, and when they are plentiful she takes them night after night."[7]

Wasson did well out of his ceremony and his association with Maria Sabina (Eva Mendez), experiencing wonders and apparent enlightenment (or at least a rip-roaring "adventure") from a single ritual, then capitalising on it with his article and the resultant prestige and celebrity as one of "the first white men in recorded history to eat the divine mushrooms" (as he excitedly tells us). The same cannot be said for his benefactor, however, after he revealed her identity against her wishes and gave her photograph to the world. Wasson's *Life* article and book sparked a huge interest in mushrooms from beatniks and hippies, which soon proved a disaster for Huautla and for María Sabina in particular, when American youth began seeking her out. To add to the throngs passing through, by 1967 more than 70 people from the US, Canada and Western Europe had taken up temporary residence in Huautla, renting cabins near the town, much to the confusion and chagrin of the locals, in order to attend her ceremonies. Matters got worse when cultural heroes like Bob Dylan and John Lennon started turning up in the small sleepy village as well, heading up a new vanguard of the dishevelled and unwashed.

When I was in Huautla for ceremonies, outside of the "tourist season" (such as it is these days, now that the hippies are gone), in November 2013, many people still remembered the influx of the 1960s and '70s and asked me if I knew John Lennon. They seemed to think that because we were both from England we must be friends, and they were unaware of his death in America 30 years before, as if that piece of news hadn't yet reached this one-street town 5,000 feet up in the cloud forests. "He was here, you know," said one elderly woman. "I saw him get off the bus and walk up the street, with his long hair and his big boots and his guitar slung over his shoulder. He hired the whole hotel just for himself ..."

The community felt itself under siege from these foreigners all wanting to experience Wasson's "wondrous mushrooms" and Sabina began to attract the attention of the police who thought that she was selling them drugs. This almost ended the historic Mazatec healing practice altogether and the community blamed Sabina. She was ostracized by them, her house was burned to the ground and her son was murdered. When anthropologist Joan Halifax visited her during the 1970s Sabina was in "a very sorry state. She was dressed in rags and covered in bite marks, having been attacked by an envious relative."[8] Before Wasson she had been a respected healer and her life was a quiet success.

As Richard Grabman writes at *The Mexfiles*[9]

> The late 1950s was the beginning of the western (or, as it was called at the time, "first world") counter-culture movement ... which romanticized the indigenous community as more "authentic" and "enlightened" and led the aficionados of a romanticized alternative lifestyle to head for Huautla de Jiménez. They had no interest in authentic or enlightening activities like bringing in María Sabina's corn or hoeing her beans but they did expect her to gratify their search for

> whatever it was that ailed them ... and to short-circuit the process to fit their own schedules ...
>
> "These young people, blonde and dark-skinned, didn't respect our customs" [remarked Maria Sabina]. "Never, as far as I remember, were the *saint children* eaten with such a lack of respect. For me it is not fun to do vigils. Whoever does it simply to feel the effects can go crazy and stay that way temporarily. Our ancestors always took the *saint children* at a vigil presided over by a Wise One ... The improper use that the young people made of the *little things* was scandalous. They obliged the authorities in Oaxaca City to intervene in Huautla ..."
>
> More than just profaning a sacred ritual, these visitors were an economic and physical drain on María Sabina (whose heirs would later remark that the Rolling Stones or Bob Dylan or one of their other wealthy visitors might have at least brought the old lady a washing machine if they expected her to do their laundry ... which she often did by hand), who never considered NOT fulfilling her duties in performing rituals and giving solace to those who asked.

Initially Sabina had been hospitable and accommodating to the "truth seekers" thronging her; perhaps she even pitied them. When Wasson had first approached her he had said he wanted to try the mushrooms so he could connect with God and, like sheep, the hippies arrived with the same agenda. Sabina was confused. Nobody in her community ate mushrooms to "find God," God was all around them – and in them – in nature, in their faith, in their way of life. As she later remarked: "Before Wasson, nobody took the children to find God. They were always taken to cure the sick."[10] So she had tried to help the visitors in their strange disconnection, their separation from God, which seemed to be the bizarre dis-ease of the West. But their lack of respect for the sacred and, ironically, their own un-God-like behavior soon caused her to question her commitment to their healing and later in life she became bitter about her misfortunes as a result of these spiritual tourists and at how Wasson had profited from her name. She also felt that the velada ceremony had been desecrated by the hedonistic and self-serving use of the mushrooms by these outsiders: "From the moment the foreigners arrived, the holy children lost their purity," she said. "They lost their force, they ruined them. Henceforth they will no longer work. There is no remedy for it."

This latter statement is not true, of course. At least, when I have attended veladas in Mexico the mushrooms ("hongos," as they are known there) work just fine and in the mushroom ceremonies I run they are effective too. It is not the mushrooms that lost their power. What happened instead is that the mushrooms stopped working *for Sabina* as a result of her own "un-Godlike" behavior. By which I mean that "magic mushrooms" are teacher plants and one of their first lessons is that we *are* God. They fill us with power and show us that we are divine and brimming with infinite potential. *There is no searching for God, as Wasson and those who came later demanded; there is only the acceptance of the God that already exists in us.* When Sabina agreed to work with Wasson on his pointless search therefore, she was in effect denying the God within him and conspiring with his sickness by enabling him to give away the power he already had to a meaningless quest. This is contrary to the job of a healer and contradicts the message of the mushrooms. In these circumstances the mushroom spirit cannot support the healer and so Sabina found herself powerless as the mushrooms left her. It was an error of judgment on her part but, of course, one which would never have happened if Wasson and his followers had not arrived in her village in the first place.

Andy Letcher summarises Wasson's contribution bluntly as follows:[11]

> He went to Mexico more as a prospector digging for gold than a philosopher looking for knowledge and truth, and ever had his eye upon how the name of Gordon Wasson would be remembered. It was this vainglorious streak that prompted him to publish his findings in *Life*, a middle-brow magazine with a massive global readership, with barely a thought for how the article might affect anyone but himself.
>
> The article itself netted Wasson the then extraordinary sum of $6000 [nearly $53,000 in today's money] … [and] within months of returning he had a meeting with top executives from the Merck Sharp & Dohme pharmaceutical company to discuss rights to the mushrooms' potential active ingredients … when Sandoz put its patented brand *Indocybin* on the market Wasson appears to have been rewarded for his part in its discovery with a directorship of one of its American subsidiaries.

As for his great contribution in attending and recording Sabina's ceremonies, Letcher tells us that:

> Knowing that *veladas* were only ever conducted for healing or to discover the whereabouts of lost or stolen possessions [Wasson] persuaded the various curanderos he did find, including Sabina, to host sessions on the pretext of concern for the well-being of his son. Later he admitted that this had been a deception performed simply to get him access to the ceremonies … [Furthermore] the picture of Mazatec religion he presented within the pages of *Life* and in his other writings was slight, superficial and in many ways inaccurate … he completely misunderstood the true nature of what Sabina was doing in her mushroom veladas … His exploits provide us with a model of how not to go about ethnographic fieldwork.

Years later, Wasson (again, in his typically understated way) would claim that "I, Gordon Wasson, am held responsible for the end of a religious practice in Mesoamerica that goes back far, for a millennia." I imagine it was said with a sense of pride as well (hopefully) as some degree of shame, but in any case (like some of the other things he wrote in his article), it was wrong. The mushroom ritual survives in Huautla, despite his efforts, though certainly it has been changed because of them.

Timothy Leary and His Merry Band of Turned-On Dropped-Out Thrill-Seekers

Timothy Francis Leary (1920–1996), an American psychologist who would later be described by President Richard Nixon as "the most dangerous man in America" (to which Leary replied, "Yeah, I have America surrounded"), picked up a copy of *Life* magazine, found Wasson's article, and changed his own life forever. Inspired by Wasson's experience, in August 1960 Leary traveled to Cuernavaca, Mexico and consumed magic mushrooms for the first time. He said later that he "learned more about ... [the] brain and its possibilities ... [and] more about psychology in the five hours after taking these mushrooms than ... in the preceding 15 years of studying and doing research."

Returning to Harvard, where he was a university professor, Leary and his associates[12] began the Harvard Psilocybin Project (HPP), a research program which set out to analyze the effects of psilocybin (the "active ingredient" of magic mushrooms) on human volunteers. Leary's Concord Prison Experiment (1961–63), part of the early HPP research, was a program to evaluate the effects of psilocybin and psychotherapy on the rehabilitation of 32 prisoners and the recidivism (return to crime) rate of those released after they had been guided through a series of trips. Records at this maximum security facility for young offenders showed an average recidivism of 64% within six months of release. In the Leary group, however, only 25% of prisoners were rearrested, six for technical parole violations and just two for new offenses. Personality test scores also showed a measurable positive change when pre-psilocybin and post-psilocybin results were compared, and many who took part spoke of profound spiritual experiences which had positively altered their lives. The experimenters concluded that a long-term reduction in recidivism rates is possible from a combination of psilocybin-assisted psychotherapy within prisons and post-release support modeled on the 12-step program used by the AA (Alcoholics Anonymous) and other "addictions Anonymous" organizations. A follow-up study published in 1999 by Rick Doblin of MAPS[13] was not quite so encouraging, pointing out flaws with the original research and with Leary's results and conclusions. It did, however, still find an improvement in recidivism rates as a consequence of Leary's approach.

Another HPP project was the Good Friday (also known as the Marsh Chapel) Experiment, which was conducted on Good Friday at Boston University's Marsh Chapel to explore the entheogenic[14] effects of psilocybin; specifically to see whether it could evoke a sense of awe and connection to God in religiously predisposed people; an apt subject for enquiry since the desire to "find God" is what had first inspired Wasson to seek out Maria Sabina and brought psilocybin to the attention of the world.

Prior to the Good Friday service, graduate divinity students were randomly divided into two groups. Half were given psilocybin while the others received a placebo (niacin – a substance which produces physiological changes but no spiritual or psychological effects and is certainly not "awe-inspiring"); those who received the placebo showed predictable physical responses which subsided over the first hour or so but reported no major shifts towards "cosmic consciousness." The psilocybin group, however, experienced effects which intensified over a number of hours and almost all participants reported profound religious experiences. One participant was the religious scholar and author Huston Smith, who later described his trip as "the most powerful cosmic homecoming I have ever experienced." In a 25-year follow-up to the experiment, all of the subjects given psilocybin reconfirmed their experience as one of "a genuine mystical nature" and characterized it as "one of the high points of their spiritual life."[15]

This experiment is widely regarded as a benchmark in providing empirical support for the notion that psychedelics (and psilocybin in particular) can facilitate religious experiences. Rick Doblin later reassessed the study and found it to be partially flawed due to certain procedural problems and the inclusion of some imprecise questions on a "mystical experience" questionnaire which participants were asked to complete. Even so, he concluded that the study cast "a considerable doubt on the assertion that mystical experiences catalyzed by drugs are in any way inferior to non-drug mystical experiences in both their immediate content and long-term effects."

In 2002 (published in 2006), a more rigorous version of the same experiment was conducted by Roland Griffiths at John Hopkins University, yielding similar results to the original. The title of Griffiths' report was unequivocal about the effects of psilocybin: *Psilocybin can occasion mystical-type experiences having a substantial and sustained personal meaning and spiritual significance.*[16] Fourteen months later, a follow-up study found that more than half of the participants continued to rate their experience of psilocybin as one of the top five most meaningful spiritual experiences of their lives; one which had increased their "personal well-being and life satisfaction."

In considering the factors at play in experiments like these (beyond the effects of psilocybin *per se*), Leary is credited with coining the term "set and setting" to describe the impact and importance of the environment and mood on encounters with teacher plants. It is doubtful, for instance, that the same level of connection with God or focus on the divine would have resulted from the Good Friday Experiment if it had been held in a funfair or an abattoir instead of a chapel.

Set refers to the state of mind with which you approach the encounter. The most important practice for anyone considering the use of mushrooms is to set an intention for the journey (e.g. "to heal" or "to overcome a creative block"). This provides a road map and a framework for the trip you are about to take. It gives it direction and purpose.

Going into a journey without intention means that you could become overwhelmed, panicked and confused, or just plain lost. As Maria Sabina once cautioned: "Whoever does it simply to feel the effects can go crazy and stay that way temporarily." Having a *reason* for taking the journey, however, means that everything you see, hear or feel relates to something definite and planned so you have some degree of control over it, a sense of direction, and a frame of reference so you can understand what's going on.

To set an intention, it is useful to have a quiet time of meditation or reflection before your trip in order to clear your mind and focus on what you want to achieve. Once the trip begins you may not always remember your intention as every question we answer for ourselves typically produces another, so some trips can be complex, depending on what you set out to explore. But clinging to intention during the journey is not important anyway, as long as you had one at the start. In shamanic terms, intention alerts the plant spirit to your purpose so it is aware of the reason for your visit (like setting the agenda for a meeting), but we do not have to continually refer to it once the spirits have been informed, any more than we have to constantly restate the agenda during a business meeting. We all know why we're here, so now we can just get on with it. It is after we return from the journey that we begin the work of understanding and integrating the information presented to us and this is when we refer to intention again. We can then interpret our experience within the framework we gave it so it makes sense to us.

Setting refers to the environment and circumstances in which the mushrooms or, indeed, any teacher plant, are taken. Always ensure that your surroundings are safe, calm, quiet, away from people who are non-participants, and away from noise and distractions. A tranquil, beautiful place in nature is better than a stuffy apartment with neighbors around, but if it has to be in an apartment, a sacred space before an altar is better than sitting in front of a TV even if it's turned off. Light some incense if you want and if you'd like to play music, give some thought to your choices. Peaceful, ambient and melodic is preferable to death metal. Your journey may be a long one (4–6 hours or more is typical with mushrooms) so prepare for it practically as well as mentally and have everything you might need to hand.

In 1962 Leary founded IFIF – the International Foundation for Internal Freedom – at Harvard to continue his research into psychedelics, healing and the expansion of consciousness. It attracted so much attention that many of the students who wanted to participate in his experiments had to be turned away as they were over-subscribed. This in turn led to a black market for psychedelics around the campus where Leary worked and was surely one of the reasons why he was fired from the prestigious university, although his termination notice focused more on his failure to deliver the lectures required by his contract. In the words of Harvard University president Nathan Pusey on May 27, 1963: "The Harvard Corporation voted, because Timothy F. Leary, lecturer on clinical psychology, has failed to keep his classroom appointments and has absented himself from Cambridge without permission, to relieve him from further teaching duty and to terminate his salary as of April 30, 1963."

With that, Leary became all at once, in the eyes of the kids, a psychedelic martyr, hip *vox pop* mushroom messiah, messenger for consciousness liberation, hippie advocate of inner-space exploration, McLuhan-inspired soundbite guru delivering quotable quotes about turning on and dropping out to a disenfranchised youth looking for leadership and, because of that, to the old guard establishment, as the "most dangerous man in America." His infamy served him well as rich fans gifted him a rambling old mansion on an estate in Millbrook where he could continue his "experiments." Leary wrote later of his time at Millbrook that "We saw ourselves as anthropologists from the 21st century inhabiting a time module set somewhere in the dark ages of the 1960s. On this space colony we were attempting to create a new paganism and a new dedication to life as art," which gives us some idea of what was actually going on there and what these experiments amounted to.

His book *The Psychedelic Experience* was published at around this time and describes the psilocybin experience as "a journey to new realms of consciousness. The scope and content of the experience is limitless but its characteristic features are the transcendence of verbal concepts, of space-time dimensions, and of the ego or identity ... Of course, the drug does not *produce* the transcendent experience. It merely acts as a chemical key – it opens the mind, frees the nervous system of its ordinary patterns and structures."

Leary's run-ins with authority and the law had been fairly frequent throughout much of his public life, although they amounted to little. That changed in December 1965 when he was arrested at the US-Mexico border for marijuana possession and sentenced to 30 years in prison, fined $30,000, and ordered to undergo psychiatric treatment. He successfully appealed the conviction on the basis that the Marijuana Tax Act was unconstitutional and in violation of the Fifth Amendment.

In December 1968 he was arrested again, this time for possession of two marijuana *roaches* – not even joints, and there is some evidence that even these were planted by the arresting officers. This time he received a 10-year sentence, with a further 10 added on for the 1965 arrest, a total of 20 years to be served consecutively. In an ironic twist of fate, on his arrival at prison he was given a psychological test used to assign inmates to appropriate work details. Having designed the test himself in his previous job he sailed through it, answering the questions in a way that made him seem conforming and conventional with a genteel interest in flowers. As a result he was assigned work as a gardener in a low-security section of prison, from which he promptly escaped and made his way to Algeria and then Switzerland.

In early 1995, Leary was diagnosed with inoperable prostate cancer and he died in May 1996, aged 75, with his death videotaped for posterity at his request. According to his son Zachary, during his final moments Leary clenched his fist and asked "Why?" then gently unclenched it and answered his own question: "Why not?" His final word, according to Zachary, was "Beautiful."

Seven grams of Leary's ashes were buried in space aboard a Pegasus rocket in April 1997. It remained in orbit for six years until it burned up in our atmosphere. More of his ashes were included in an art installation at the Burning Man festival in 2015. They were burned along with the installation on September 6.

Terence McKenna and His "Mushroom Intelligentsia"

Terence Kemp McKenna (1946–2000) was an American ethnobotanist and author who came to be known, amongst other things (and not entirely accurately), as "the Timothy Leary of the '90s," and (more accurately) as a "charismatic talking head" and the "intellectual voice of rave culture."

In 1965 he enrolled as a student at the University of California, Berkley, where he developed his interest in psychedelics, during a stage in his life he later called his "opium and kabbala phase." In 1971, after the partial completion of his studies,[17] he traveled with his brother Dennis and three friends to the Colombian Amazon in search of *oo-koo-he* (ayahuasca), a plant preparation containing dimethyltryptamine (DMT).[18] His focus changed almost immediately at La Chorrera, however, when he stumbled across a field of *Psilocybe cubensis* mushrooms and embarked upon a bizarre new experiment, where he and his brother essentially attempted, via ayahusaca, to bond the spirit of magic mushrooms to their neural DNA using vocal techniques they believed had been taught to them by (a possibly alien intelligence living within) the mushrooms. Quite.

The McKennas convinced themselves that if they were successful the practice would give them access to the collective memory of all mankind and allow them to manifest in three-dimensional reality the alchemical Philosopher's Stone, which they saw as a "hyper-dimensional union of spirit and matter."

Years later, Dennis wrote about the experiment in his book, *The Brotherhood of the Screaming Abyss*[19] that "Whether the ideas that seized us over those days were telepathically transmitted by the mushroom, or by a mantis-like entity on the bridge of a starship in geosynchronous orbit above the Amazon (which we considered), or created within our own minds, I'll never know." At the time however, while gluttonously ripped on vast amounts of ayahuasca and shrooms, everything seemed cool and groovy so it was just natural and obvious to go along with an experiment which "The Teacher" (either the mushroom spirit or an entity conjured up by the mushrooms) had suggested to him. "Or I believed so anyway, in my state of hypermania."

> The goal [was] to fabricate an actual object within the alchemical crucible of my body. This thing would be a fusion of mind and matter created by the fourth-dimensional rotation of the metabolizing psilocybin and its exteriorization, or "freezing," into a physical object. Such an object would be the ultimate artifact. It would be the philosopher's stone, or the UFO space-time machine, or the resurrection body – all these things being conceptualizations of the same thing. The Teacher was downloading the blueprints for building

> a hyper-dimensional vehicle out of the 4-D transformation of my own DNA interlaced with the DNA of a mushroom. But not just blueprints alone. I was also getting step-by-step instructions on how to build this transcendental object …
>
> To put that another way, what the Teacher had transmitted was a set of procedures for creating, and then fixing, the mercury of my own consciousness, fused with the four-dimensionally transformed psilocybin-DNA complex of a living mushroom.

Huh? What does any of that mean? "I might ask the same question now," says McKenna, "but at the time it was perfectly clear." The idea was to manifest "a hyper-dimensional object" dragged here now from the end of time, made of mushrooms, ayahuasca and McKenna DNA, welded together by the sound of his voice while ripped on a huge dose of psilocybin and ayahuasca, the purpose of which was to bring about the end of time. This is what McKenna meant by the philosopher's stone. Once manifested, he would be instructed in its usage by "some infinitely wise, infinitely adept fellow member of the hyperspatial community; of that I feel sure." This action will be that of humankind taking "the keys to galactarian citizenship. I speculate that we will be the first five human beings to be instructed in its use. Our mission will be to selectively disseminate it to the rest of humanity."

To create this wondrous object it was necessary to first make a ceremonial circle and within it place a mushroom which would act as a "receiving template," along with some ayahuasca and the chrysalis of a blue morpho butterfly. Then, kneeling together in the circle, each participant would drink a cup of ayahuasca, eat mushrooms, and climb into their hammocks to await the inevitable miracle.

The anticipated result "didn't happen, of course … because it *could* not happen; such an event would have violated the laws of physics." But what did happen was perhaps even stranger and even more wondrous ... Perhaps.

> I felt I'd manifested a kind of internalized entity, an intelligence now inside me that had access to a cosmic database. I could hear and speak to this oracular presence. I could ask it questions – and get answers. As I explained to Terence, the oracle could be queried by prefacing the question with the name "Dennis." For instance, "Dennis, what is the name of this plant?" And the oracle would instantly respond with a scientific name. Terence soon learned the oracle could also be addressed as "McKenna." Something very peculiar was going on ...
>
> Shortly thereafter I lost my glasses, or rather, I hurled them into the jungle, along with my clothes, in one of my bouts of ecstasy. My blurred vision for the next few weeks surely playing into my estrangement from reality. When I tried to share our wondrous discovery with the others, they were underwhelmed. Vanessa, our resident skeptic, asked some mathematical questions of the oracle, and it was flummoxed, or it gave answers we couldn't verify. Nevertheless, Terence and I were utterly convinced we had succeeded. We were sure that a wave of gnosis was sweeping the world with the advancing dawn line; people were waking up to find themselves, as Terence put it, "pushing off into a telepathic ocean whose name was that of its discoverer: Dennis McKenna."

If these sound like the ravings of a madman or of someone who has at least taken too many drugs, in fairness, Dennis probably wouldn't disagree with you now, not with the benefit of age, maturity and hindsight. And yet, this bizarre episode and the bizarre musings on mushrooms which followed it, have given rise to a number of popular theories that the "hippie intelligentsia" fell for hook, line and sinker, baffled as they were (and in some cases still are) by the McKenna's bullshit.

One of these noodlings is the so-called "stoned monkey" hypothesis. In it Terence proposes that human beings owe their very existence to magic mushrooms. The theory goes like this: as the North African jungles receded toward the end of the most recent Ice Age, giving way to grasslands, our primate ancestors left their forests and took up a nomadic hunter-gatherer lifestyle, following the trails of grazing cattle and eating what they could along the way. Among the new items in their diet were psilocybin mushrooms growing in the dung of the cattle herds. And with that, voila, enlightened apes.

The evolutionary changes caused by the introduction of magic mushrooms into the primate diet were, according to McKenna, the development of language in an attempt to communicate and understand the common messages, motifs and symbols that the mushrooms presented and, as a result of that, community as people united under a common idiom. With community an infrastructure developed, leading to institutions, laws, and to "civilization." Spirituality and then religions also developed as a way for our ancestors to maintain a connection to the divine world that the mushrooms had shown them.

To some this may sound like radical stuff. Certainly it is a new take on the accepted rhetoric about evolution trotted out by Darwinists. But in fact it's not that novel, especially when we remember that Wasson received a similar revelation from the mushrooms quite a few decades before Terence. As he stated in his *Life* article: "In man's evolutionary past ... there must have come a moment in time when he discovered the secret of the hallucinatory mushrooms. Their effect on him, as I see it, could only have been profound, a detonator to new ideas. For the mushrooms revealed to him worlds beyond the horizons known to him, in space and time, even worlds on a different plane of being, a heaven and perhaps a hell. For the credulous primitive mind, the mushrooms must have reinforced mightily the idea of the miraculous ... one is emboldened to the point of asking whether they may not have planted in primitive man the very idea of god."

Maybe there's something in the mushrooms that brings us to this collective realization, or some ancestral memory locked in our DNA that is liberated through the effects of psilocybin so we remember what happened way back in our history when we first began to eat these mushrooms. A more prosaic explanation for why McKenna came up with the same idea as Wasson, however, is simply that McKenna "borrowed" the exiting theory, added a few big words to it and passed it off as his own. It wouldn't be the only time.

This romantic idyll of happy brainy trippy monkeys collapsed about 12,000 years ago, McKenna continues, as further climate changes removed mushroom from the human diet. Because of this we reverted back to our more primitive and brutish natures, giving rise to the world of today. The solution seems clear, then: to solve our modern problems of conflict and alienation an "archaic revival" is needed, where mushrooms and other teacher plants become a regular part of our lives once again. Speaking in *High Times* magazine, McKenna added:

> The presence of psychedelic substances in the diet of early human beings created a number of changes in our evolutionary situation. When a person takes small amounts of psilocybin visual acuity improves. They can actually see slightly better, and this means that animals allowing psilocybin into their food chain would have increased hunting success, which means increased food supply, which means increased reproductive success, which is the name of the game in evolution. It is the organism that manages to propagate itself numerically that is successful ... At slightly higher doses of psilocybin there is sexual arousal, erection, and everything that goes under the term arousal of the central nervous system. Again, a factor

which would increase reproductive success is reinforced.

But where did these mushrooms come from? Was there an even greater purpose in their interaction with us, beyond mere accident? Is there something more to this? According to McKenna, yes. In his view, psilocybin mushrooms are a species of advanced alien intelligence which arrived on this planet as spores that migrated through space and are now attempting to establish a symbiotic relationship with human beings.

Surprisingly, perhaps, this is not as far-fetched as it sounds, and in fact there is a long history of such thought not only among philosophers and hippies but scientists too. Even Francis Crick, the discoverer of the structure of DNA, arrived at the conclusion that life – and DNA, the beginnings of life and evolution – could not possibly have arisen randomly and by chance on this planet but must have been sent here deliberately by another race as a seed bank in a sort of interplanetary ark, for motives unclear. He called his theory "directed panspermia," the idea that life on Earth was purposefully seeded and is perhaps still overseen and directed by a higher alien intelligence.

"As I understand the Crick theory of panspermia," said McKenna, "it's a theory of how life spread through the universe. What I was suggesting ... is that *intelligence* – not life, but *intelligence* – may have come here in this spore-bearing life form ... As far as the role of the psilocybin mushroom, or its relationship to us and to intelligence, this is something that we need to consider ... Few people are in a position to judge its extra-terrestrial potential because few people in the orthodox sciences have ever experienced the full spectrum of psychedelic effects that are unleashed. One cannot find out whether or not there's an extra-terrestrial intelligence inside the mushroom unless one is willing to take the mushroom."

To some, thinking like this is revolutionary as well as evolutionary; it gets us outside of our box of narrow, standardised consensus thought and leads us into new possibilities as an expansion of our creativity and potential. The world, after all, was never changed, and nothing positive, new or progressive ever came from sheeple (even if they call themselves "scientists") repeating the same old paradigms and dogmas (whether of flawed Darwinian evolutionary theory – explain flowers or the eye, show us the fossil record – or Creationism) from a basis of fear (of losing tenure, research grants, respectability, face ... etc.). Left to sheeple-scientists the Earth would still be flat with the Sun revolving around it at the center of a finite universe. Left to sheeple-theologians the Earth would have been created in seven days with dinosaur fossils put here as a test of faith by a potty, piss-taking God. Stuck in the mire of dogma, neither side is capable of advancing our understanding of what it means to be human, to be alive. Only outsiders can do that. It is always the revolutionaries, the heretics and visionaries who really change the world because they dare to stand up and speak for something new. We can appreciate McKenna for this and for the (partial) creativity of his theory.

To others, such theories are magical thinking which come from their own basis in fear and limitations; stemming in a way, that is, from a belief that human beings are incapable of progression on their own terms, of inventing and re-inventing themselves and of taking their own evolutionary steps but must turn in prayer, supplication or awe to gods or, in this case, aliens: an advanced race of others – the "Senders of the Mushrooms" – who will child-mind us, intervene in our fuck-ups and save us from ourselves. This abdication of power, responsibility and the will to self-government is the basis of all religions which rely on a "sky-father-saviour-God" to manage, reward and punish us, and also the basis for our repressive systems of laws and government. It also implies a certain arrogance which is all too common in human thinking: that we are somehow so special and precious to the universe that gods and aliens are putting all their resources into our advancement and salvation. Really? You *really* believe that's the case? Or is it time we got over ourselves?

In fact, during a mushroom ceremony I ran in New Zealand, following McKenna's theory, I asked the mushrooms where they came from – which planet – and why. This, almost verbatim, is what they said:

> You humans are so arrogant. You actually believe that the universe assembled itself in some grand campaign to liberate and enlighten you; that kindly benevolent races a billion years more advanced than you are watching your progress with an all-engrossing interest and sending you "space spores" across thousands of light years to save you and help you create a new utopia so they can welcome you into their space fraternity when you are ready to join them. Ask yourself: would you bother traveling even a few feet to assist a nest of termites in their evolution so they could be more like you? Yet that's what you seriously imagine the "galactic federation" is doing for you …
>
> We [the mushrooms] did not come here from any *other* planet to assist you. We *are* the planet. *This planet*. We have always been here – for billions of years before you. It is human beings who have just arrived. We fashioned you from clay, dust and dirt, as our playthings. As an experiment. Just as we've done many times before, with all the civilizations before you, who also came and went, who rose and fell and returned to dirt to become the mulch and the soil that we grow in.

They have a point. And it's not such an off-the-wall idea – that mushrooms are the voice of the planet – or, at least, I'm not the only one to have had it. McKenna himself once said that "the planet has a kind of intelligence, it can actually open a channel of communication with an individual human being." And then there's this:

> Consider this thou new made Mushroom man
> Thy life's a blast, a bubble, and a span
> And thou with all thy gorgeous trappings gay
> Art but a mouldring lump of guilded clay.
> (John Taylor, 1639)

This is not to dismiss McKenna's take on the panspermia theory entirely. It is possible of course that the universe *is* alive, aware and interactive in a way that human beings are too stupid to comprehend, so billions of years ago – either by design or by accident – comets or starships may well have crashed to Earth carrying the seeds of intelligence from other planets. And maybe they did influence the evolution of ours, creating the intelligent, self-regulating homeostatic system that we now call *Gaia*[20] but that in no way implies that all of this was done for human benefit.

Another of McKenna's mushroom-inspired ideas was one he called Novelty Theory or Timewave Zero, which claims to predict the ebb and flow of the universe according to its various qualities tending towards either habit or novelty. Habit is repetitive and conservative while novelty is creative and progressive and the universe is a kind of engine producing both. As novelty increases so does complexity. We can see the basis of this idea in the La Chorrera experiment where time for the McKennas became an interplay of opposites (expansion/contraction), experienced personally and uniquely as the driving force of creation.

McKenna eventually worked out a mathematical formula to explain his Novelty Theory and developed Timewave Zero software to graph it on a computer. To cut a long story short, the software showed that time was speeding up and that infinite novelty would be reached on a specific date since the universe appeared to have a "teleological attractor" situated at the end of time which increases interconnectedness, eventually creating a singularity of infinite complexity. McKenna called it "the transcendental object at the end of time."

> The universe is not being pushed from behind. The universe is being pulled from the future toward a goal that is as inevitable as a marble reaching the bottom of a bowl when you release it up near the rim. If you do that, you know the marble will roll down the side of the bowl, down, down, down – until eventually it comes to rest at the lowest energy state, which is the bottom of the bowl. That's precisely my model of human history. I'm suggesting that the universe is pulled toward a complex attractor that exists ahead of us in time, and that our ever-accelerating speed through the phenomenal world of connectivity and novelty is based on the fact that we are now very, very close to the attractor.

According to McKenna, December 21, 2012 was the point at which maximum novelty would be experienced, an event he described as a "concrescence", a "tightening gyre" with everything flowing together so that "the laws of physics are obviated, the universe disappears, and what is left is the tightly bound plenum, the monad able to express itself for itself, rather than only able to cast a shadow into physics as its reflection ... It will be the entry of our species into hyperspace but it will appear to be the end of physical laws, accompanied by the release of the mind into the imagination."

Which is more-or-less what he said about his "experiments" at La Chorrera as well, when he thought he would stop time and save our species by manifesting the Philosopher's Stone (megalomania anyone?), and that never happened either. Nobody vanished into hyperspace as a result of either event, nor do we see much "mind-releasing" going on in the world or an exponential growth in imagination and new creative thought.

Others have criticized Novelty Theory for its rather arbitrary dating of the end of time. The Timewave Zero program itself produced a date for the "concrescence" of November 2012 but McKenna didn't like that so he changed it to December 2012 to make it coincide with the Mayan calendar because, er, reasons (one of them being that it just looked prettier). The British mathematician Mathew Watkins of Exeter University also weighed in to note that there are various mathematical flaws in the construction of McKenna's timewave and when these are ironed out a much more trivial and uninteresting waveform is created. In other words, McKenna was wrong again.

Probably McKenna's most useful *actual* contribution to our modern work with mushrooms, in fact, is not his wordy but unworkable theories but something much more down-to-earth and practical in that he developed the first, best and most reliable technique for cultivating magic mushrooms and published this in his 1976 book *Psilocybin: Magic Mushroom Grower's Guide*. As ethnobotanist Jonathan Ott commented, "The new technique involved the use of ordinary kitchen implements and for the first time the layperson was able to produce a potent entheogen in his own home, without access to sophisticated technology, equipment or chemical supplies." Nowadays, however, even this is somewhat redundant since complete mushroom grow kits can now be bought easily and cheaply over the internet which usually produce a reliable crop of effective mushrooms, but it should still be remembered as an achievement of its time.

McKenna died from brain cancer on April 3, 2000, at the age of 53. Timothy Leary had described him as "one of the five or six most important people on the planet." Jerry Garcia of the "head" band The Grateful Dead added gushingly but far from accurately that he was "the only person who has made a serious effort to objectify the psychedelic experience." But maybe the last word here should go to *Wired* magazine which described McKenna as "a charismatic talking head." His theories may not amount to much and, all things considered, while he had a lot of words to say which all sounded "brainy, eloquent, and hilarious" (according to *Wired*), there is not much substance to them and nor is there much genuine guidance or useful advice contained within them for safely and successfully working with mushrooms.

The Mushroom Men: An Evaluation

So, all things considered, what are we to make of these "mushroom men" singularly and as a collective whose words inform our age?

Wasson. While you have to admire (even grudgingly) a banker (Wasson was a vice president at J. P. Morgan & Co) who is prepared to trip the light fantastic at a mushroom ceremony in Mexico and then have the balls to write about it (I can't imagine that happening nowadays), we have to put his accomplishments into perspective. Yes, he brought mushrooms to the widespread attention of the West with his article in *Life*. On the other hand, he also betrayed the woman who introduced him to these mushrooms, took credit from her as if mushrooms were his invention, and published an article that made him a small fortune while contributing to her alienation from the village she lived in, the pollution (spiritual and otherwise) of an entire town as the Great Unwashed descended on it looking for a quick mushroom high, and almost led to the end of mushroom ceremonies altogether and the destruction of a centuries-old culture of healing. Nor did he seem overly apologetic about it. As he said: "I, Gordon Wasson, am held responsible for the end of a religious practice in Mesoamerica that goes back far, for a millennia." And, for all this, the article that resulted from his "great adventure" wasn't entirely accurate either. So was it all worth it? You decide.

Leary. While Leary began his psychedelic career with (and on) mushrooms, he was hardly loyal to them and in fact he is probably best remembered as the "High Priest" of LSD. An advocate of getting wasted and "losing one's mind" in general (an approach he typically justified by reference to pseudo-psychology and pseudo-spirituality) his greatest advocacy was probably the Leary brand itself. The soundbite king of the '60s with his big smile and his Irish blarney confused the matter no end for genuine seekers of self-discovery, mushroom healing and communion with something wiser, older and greater than themselves. Under his cultural leadership mushrooms became a mélange of revolution, defiance, "pushing back boundaries," flowers poked into rifle barrels, "freeing the mind" (from what? How?), Millbrook orgies, drug-fueled days and up-all-nights, persecution by the law, daring prison escapes, beaches in Mexico, turning on in artsy New York apartments, a string of wives and the courting of fortunes. All of it screamed Leary, very little of it whispered spirit, and none of it bore any resemblance to a traditional mushroom healing ceremony.

To balance the equation, he gave us the useful concepts of "set" and "setting" (not entirely unknown to shamans, of course, since they had already been running mushroom ceremonies for millennia before Leary came along to tell them how to do it properly) and his early work with the HPP in prisons and university chapels hinted at the potential of psilocybin for healing and spiritual communion. But then his interest wavered (not helped by his university sacking) and he seized on the next great adventure, as Leary seemed almost always inclined to do, whether it was psychedelic research or the next woman to bed.[21] His early work showed promise and gave us something useful to think about but then Leary seemed to get in his own way (or maybe he dropped out of his way and just allowed the fun to flow), leaving us with a confused pop-psychology take on mushrooms overshadowed by the man himself.

McKenna. If Leary was the soundbite king of the '60s, addressing the kids with the pop-flowery language of his times, McKenna "the Timothy Leary of the '90s" used this as a board to kick off from. His audience, by contrast (or at least my impression of it), was the new wave intelligentsia of the '80s and '90s who used "drugs" to be seen as "relevant," "streetwise," "hip" and "aware," when they weren't attending Basquiat openings, dissecting the New York Times style section over breakfast croissants or sipping champagne at fashion shows. McKenna the nice, clever middle-class boy, sanitised drug-taking for them and made it not only safe but hot – and cool – all at the same time. Rather than "keeping it street" (which Leary had at least had the grace to do), McKenna's word-heavy lectures, meandering yet bizarrely somehow on-point, are worth revisiting later for post-shock-and-awe analysis of the Desert Storm of his barrage of words. Doing so, one becomes aware of just how many obscure and multi-syllabic words there are in the English language and how many can be crammed into a single sentence, as well as how much poetry can be left floating in empty air, and how little content it all contained. His theories – either proven wrong (Timewave Zero) or hijacked from others and incapable of proof either way (stoned monkey, panspermia) – became the stuff (or maybe the fluff) of "legendary dinner parties" where middlebrow liberals would debate "the coming singularity" and "the entheogenically-inspired evolution of apes," as if it mattered or meant something, while passing the port, the brie and the fungi.

To be fair, McKenna also stood for a more considered relationship with psychedelics than Leary's sloganizing. He at least encouraged us to *think* about our experience and give it a context in our lives. Certainly he advocated excess and called for the taking of "heroic doses"[22] but he also proposed a time for reflection so that people could evaluate what the mushrooms had taught them. The fact that in McKenna's case this led to some strange conclusions and bizarre attempts to manifest a philosopher's stone out of thin air and then end time should really – and I mean genuinely – be regarded as neither here nor there since the information we receive from mushrooms, the understanding we derive from them and the integration of this data into our lives is individual and unique to us all.

Collectively, I would argue, these three have left us confused about the nature of mushrooms and our relationship to them, partly because we are seeing the mushrooms through their eyes and conflating the messenger with the message. If we are Leary-ites we will receive the "mood" of mushrooms as one of hedonistic flower power hippie-rebellion (not so much activism as a lazy pot-head-in-the-clouds excuse to do nothing except eat more mushrooms because "change your mind and the system will take care of itself"). If we are McKenna-ites our predominant experience of mushrooms may be what they can contribute to making us look sophisticated and clever during deep and ultimately meaningless faux-philosophical "debates" and one-line postings on Facebook. Even Wasson, who at least attended and described a real mushroom ceremony (which none of the others did), gave us errors in his account and his "great adventure" is more than tinged with self-centeredness: to have the experience no matter what.

Today, if you ask someone for their views on mushrooms, especially if they have never tried psilocybin themselves or attended a ceremony and are given to lazily repeating the bullshit peddled by tabloids, you are first likely to end up with a cliché about people jumping off buildings thinking they can fly.[23] If they are more positive towards mushrooms, however, but again have little experience personally you are more likely to get a received wisdom word muesli based on the writings of these three. Through them you'll soon get familiar with and pretty blasé about some otherwise off-the-wall concepts, including "saviour aliens," "evolution from outer space," "peaceniks and hippies and rainbow children," "stoned apes," "flower power," "rave culture," "techno," "experiments in expanded consciousness," "taking the heroic dose" and of course, the repeated-verbatim "wisdom" of Leary, McKenna and Wasson themselves. The words "healing," "ceremony," and "sacred" will rarely enter into it. Which is a pity, since these are the words which really apply, and the true reason for the shamanic use of mushrooms.

So let's restore the balance now and look at how *shamans* work with mushrooms as allies for teaching and healing, and how you might do so too so you get more from your investment in the experience than just "tripping out."

2

Ceremonies with Shrooms

Le llevan ahí donde Dios está,
They carry you there where God is.
R. Gordon Wasson

As we saw in the last chapter, Wasson, who plays such a large part, sadly, in informing us about what to expect from healing with mushrooms, was wrong about quite a few things. Contrary to the quote above, for example, the mushrooms do not carry you to God – an idea which totally confused Maria Sabina and the people of her town – they are used for direct practical healing not siteseeing trips to paradise. Secondly, they do not necessarily take *you* anywhere since in some traditional ceremonies the patient/participant did not even eat the mushrooms, only the shaman did so he could talk with the spirits to diagnose your problem and then cure it with their assistance. Thirdly, Wasson is wrong in his observation that the mushrooms are "always counted in pairs." Since he only attended a few ceremonies with one *curandera* in one town in Mexico, how would he know? If it takes just one exception to disprove a rule, having attended ceremonies with a few different mushroom shamans, including in Huautla de Jimenez, I can tell you that mushrooms are not even "always" served in pairs in the very town where Wasson took his.

Serving the Mushrooms

So how do you serve mushrooms? The answer is almost "however you want." Like you, I have read the accounts of "expert" anthropologists and New Age "gurus" who explain how it is vital that the mushrooms are picked and served by virgins, always in pairs/threes/five at a time, on plates which are always red/blue/porcelain/wood and patterned with ponies or daisies. Take it from me (or go ahead and find out by attending ceremonies yourself) that this is nonsense. In parts of Eastern Europe, mushrooms are not even served whole but prepared and stored in vodka (whatever number fills the bottle), staining the alcohol blue. The liquor is then drunk by the glass and the flesh of the mushrooms eaten (a practice I have also encountered in Wales). In Siberia, the red and white *Amanita muscaria* (fly agaric) is cut into slices and boiled in milk which is then drunk and the softened mushrooms eaten. In Juxtlahuaca, Mexico, shamans grind the mushrooms into a fine powder and brew a tea with it (again, a method I have also experienced in Wales). In other places in Mexico, including Huautla, the mushrooms are served on a plate with a few cacao beans. The number of mushrooms and beans vary according to the shaman, the size of the mushrooms and the time of year (mushrooms are more potent in Mexico in June and July, so at ceremonies later in the year more will be needed to achieve the same effect) but at *none* of the events I attended were the mushrooms served in pairs or delivered to me by a virgin, and the plates were disposable cardboard.

Research published by Elisa Guerra-Doce, an archaeologist at the University of Valladolid in Spain, shows that plant-assisted altered states of consciousness were nearly ubiquitous in societies throughout history. Of 488 human societies she found that 437 or 90% of them incorporated altered states of consciousness into their fundamental belief systems.

> People used ... hallucinogens derived from the San Pedro cactus in the Andes as far back as 10,600 years, hallucinogenic mescal beans in Texas and northern Mexico 11,000 years ago, and peyote from between 9,000 and 5,600 years ago. People also apparently got high on opium as the poppy was

> domesticated in the western Mediterranean 8,000 years ago; the mildly stimulating (among other benefits) coca leaves for tea and chewing in South America from at least 6,000 BCE; cannabis (marijuana) in central Asia 7,000 years ago and hallucinogenic nightshade all over the world as long ago as 5,000 years. There were tobacco in the New World 4,000 years ago, hallucinogenic yopo snuff from the New World more than 4,000 years ago, and hallucinogenic mushrooms from various places and times around the world.[24]

That being the case we should expect some variation in mushroom preparation and methods of consumption around the world, and this of course is what we find. As with all genuine ceremonies, there is also considerable room for creative input on the part of the shaman, the key thing being guidance from spirit and absolute faith in the mushroom as an aware sentient ally which has the patient's best interests at heart. In most circumstances where the shaman wishes the participant to feel an effect from the mushrooms he will administer 3.5 to 5gms of active material (3.5gms being a reasonable beyond-threshold dose and 5gms giving a deeper and more intense journey) but *how* this is administered and how many mushrooms it takes does not matter greatly.

In the ceremonies I run, we measure each dose on a scale to ensure fairness for all participants but, in truth, this could easily be done by eye, sizing up the mushrooms to give a more-or-less equal portion for each person. A second dose can be given later if the person needs it. I serve my mushrooms on a plate (any plate is fine), along with cacao beans and a glass of good tequila, alcohol (and, I suspect, chocolate) being a good way to liberate the potency of the mushrooms.

Ceremonies in Huautla, Mexico

As Letcher informs us, "To pick a mushroom at random in Mexico is to stand a very good chance of picking a hallucinogenic one, which is probably why it is the one part of the world where there is a genuinely old tradition of psilocybin mushroom usage," and, again: "Perhaps uniquely in the world, there exists in the region we now call Mexico a genuine history of intentional psilocybin mushroom consumption that extends back at least five thousand years to the time of the Spanish conquest but may go back much further." Mexico is the "ground zero" of magic mushrooms. It is also a country in which I have experienced mushroom ceremonies, having journeyed there and to Huautla, Oxaca – the "ground zero" of the "ground zero" of magic mushrooms, birthplace of Maria Sabina and the town where Wasson attended his ceremonies – specifically to join the rituals. To illustrate the similarities (and differences) in the shamanic approach to such events, I share here my impressions of two curanderas and their modern day ceremonies. This is what you'll find if you journey there yourself.

Getting to Huautla

The road out of Oaxaca, where you must catch the bus to Huautla de Jimenez from the Maria Sabina bus station, winds – and winds – up – and up – *and up* – then down for five hours until it reaches the town which, in the Mazatec language is known as *Tejao* (Eagle's Nest), denoting its location at the top of a peak high up in a cloud forest. *De Jiménez* was added later in honor of General Mariano Jiménez, the first governor of the state of Oaxaca.

Our small bus of 13 people, two chickens, a dog and a goat drives through clouds, sometimes clinging to a cliff face so we don't drop off the edge of the world. The landscape is littered with cacti taller than trees and the road smells sometimes of salvia tea, sometimes oddly of fish. A kid behind me screams for an hour. Her mother is totally unconcerned. Clearly not an English speaker and/or poor enough not to care how she dresses, she wears a distressed t-shirt three sizes smaller than her child-bearing frame, emblazoned with the legend "Peace Music ... Eagle." I listen to the radio, counting the number of "corazones" (hearts) that crop up during each song. I give up after three hours of Spanish crooning and 220 corazones. The Spanish love a heart in their songs, whether broken, lost, achy-breaky, wounded, tortured, or once-in-a-while even happy.

The road bottoms out sometimes into valleys with dry or still-flowing rivers; then we begin a new ascent past occasional roadside shrines, mostly comprised of flowers, to praise an ever-present God, a long-lost son, or a timeless *apu* (mountain spirit). It starts to get humid as we drive through the forest in rain and fog. With a visibility of about 20 yards our driver is still doing 50km an hour around hairpin bends with a million mile drop on each side of the road. His confidence is the only thing between us and death. He is fearless, young and knows the road but more importantly he has a Virgin de Guadalupe prayer card stuck to his windshield which is our protection and our salvation. A town appears almost without warning and we skid to a halt opposite a funeral parlor. We're in Huautla de Jimenez and it's raining.

"It's always raining," says a stranger who meets us from the bus and takes us to "Casa Julia" without even being asked. We're the only gringos on the bus – the only gringos in town at this time of year – and there's only one place we could possibly be going so that's where he takes us. Julia – Julieta Casimiro – whose house it is, has achieved a small degree of fame in Mexico, and outside it, as she is a member of the International Council of Thirteen Indigenous Grandmothers, "an alliance of thirteen women elders from across the globe that was organized to uphold indigenous practices and ceremonies and affirm the right to use plant medicines free of legal restriction" according to academic Suzanne Bouclin. The council meets every six months, visiting each other's country, during which they wear traditional dress and hold a seven-day prayer vigil. In July 2008 the council met in Rome to address the Vatican regarding a Papal Bull of 1493 that authorised the conversion to Christianity of the indigenous people of the newly discovered Americas. The grandmothers laid a "flag of peace and conciliation" in front of Saint Peter's Basilica, lit smudging incense and prayed. The Vatican declined to receive them.

Julia is friendly enough when we meet her; tiny, about 4 feet 8 inches tall, always giggling and throwing her head back to reveal a single tooth. One of the requirements of being a Grandmother is that you must actually be a grandmother so, while it's difficult to guess her age, it must be way past 60 as Omar, her son, himself looks as if he's approaching 40. She has photos on her wall of herself with the Dalai Lama and other dignitaries, next to jars of mushrooms preserved in honey and magic potions in bottles. In one of them there is a snake.

Omar tells us there will be a *hongo* (mushroom) ceremony tomorrow night so we must not eat meat or frijoles (beans), but rice, any fruit or veg and spice is okay. The diet to be followed with different plants varies, not just according to the plant and the place but also the shaman. In the Amazon, for example, during ayahuasca retreats it is not usual to eat meat (especially pork), though fish may be okay, but certainly not spice and most vegetables and fruits are also out. In Mexico and with mushrooms, and with this shaman at least, it is different.

We go for a little walk. Looking at a map of Huautla in a guidebook, the scale of the town is measured in feet as opposed to other towns and cities which might be measured in miles. On the page it looked like the town was a few thousand yards maximum from beginning to end and contained only about 20 buildings of interest, including a post office, a bank and three hotels, one of them listed as "for emergencies only." On the ground it doesn't look a lot bigger. We walk from one end to the other in about five minutes. It's enough to get soaked and catch a glimpse of a run-down third-world village with dogs and chickens wandering the streets or hiding in closed shop doorways out of the mud and water flowing past them. A coffin-maker is one of the few stores open, its doors pulled wide to reveal a small workshop with a dozen coffins made up and ready to go and work being done on two more by a carpenter who looked ready for one himself. Business was booming for some in this town.

Ceremonies with Julieta Casimiro of the International Council of Thirteen Indigenous Grandmothers

The mushroom ceremony, when it came, took place in a basement chapel built into a hillside below Julia's house. It began with a *limpia* (ritual cleansing) using the stems of *ruda* (the rue plant) to sprinkle us with holy water. Then the smoke of burning copal was passed over us and Julia made prayers to the Virgin for us to be healed, finally lighting candles on the biggest altar I have ever seen. It was massive; about 20 feet long and six feet high. In the center a five feet tall by three feet deep cabinet housed an almost life-size statue of the Virgin de Guadalupe. Around it, intermingled with other statues of the saints, religious pictures, rattles, paintings, prayer books, incense, drums and shamanic paraphernalia were six huge vases of fresh flowers and in front of it nine white candles. She lit two – one for each of us in attendance – and then climbed into her "cockpit": a sort of "cot" on the floor which had a bench of cushions behind it and another smaller altar in front of it containing medicines, copal, etc., which Julia sat between like a jet pilot, an astronaut or an infant.

She wore a bandana and her hair was loose and long now, braided almost down to her waist, but she wore no special ritual clothes. From the cockpit she handed us a plate each, holding five large *cubensis* mushrooms, dirt and all, as if they had just been pulled up fresh from the mud, and two cacao beans (in the old Mayan ceremonies, mushrooms were always taken with cacao, she said), and a dab of honey if we wanted it. They tasted of nothing much, maybe a little earthy, but they felt like flesh as I chewed them, though not human flesh, more like fish.[25]

She began praying, using a rosary. It seemed like 100 prayers and went on for an hour – to San Antonio, San Pedro, San Pablo, San Martin ... She had statues of all of them too, each one three feet tall or taller, on her altar – and always to "Santa Maria, madre de dios." When she finished she turned out the little electric light in her cockpit, blew out the candles then lit another solitary candle which would illuminate the rest of the ceremony.

The entire event was run from the cockpit. She never moved from it once. For four hours she prayed, reciting words from ragged and frayed typed sheets on her cockpit altar, illuminated by her head torch. She also sang, mumbling songs that sounded part-icaro, part-lullaby but were mostly conventional hymns like those you would hear in any church, which were again read aloud from a song book she held in her torchlight.

At times she knelt before her smaller altar, arms outstretched, beseeching the Virgin and praying to her statue on the bigger altar. That was her only real movement during the evening though, and there was little interaction with us or on our behalf. At one point she did speak directly to Bodge (the woman I was with), telling her "You are the same as me except for one thing – you are a feminist." She didn't elaborate further so what she meant by that was never made clear. It should be noted though that Bodge is not and has never been a feminist; she's actually more of a pragmatist. Another time she made prayers for "Mi hermana desde Londres con triste" ("my sister from London who is sad"). Clearly she meant Bodge again, although Bodge had said nothing about feeling sad and actually seemed quite chirpy, so the purpose of the prayer was confusing. She made another prayer for "mi hermano con gripe," as I had a cold and felt a bit sick.

Her "performance" was technical more than inspired. There was none of the spirit-led steam of consciousness poetry of a

Maria Sabina ceremony; it was more as if she was reading from a manual – which, indeed, she was in the form of hymn books and prayer sheets – and more concerned with "following the script" than allowing the spirit to guide her.

She was attentive enough. If either of us coughed or moved abruptly she would ask "es todo bien?" (Is everything okay?) but even this felt odd. Every other shaman I'd been in ceremony with (probably close to 30) wouldn't need to ask, they would *know* based on the energy of the room. Perhaps it was her advanced age, perhaps she had been dynamic and powerful in her prime, but it felt lacking in her now.

"You cannot be a good curandera without an ego," writes Elizabeth de la Portilla, in *They All Want Magic: Curanderas and Folk Healing*. "One half of calling oneself a curandera is to claim the status for yourself ... the other half is to be acknowledged as one by the community." Disappointingly, it was as if, now at least, Julia had either relinquished her power (ego) and was going through the motions of healing or that she was so secure in her ego that she felt she could just coast it and no one would notice or care. But for my part, if I was her "community" that night, I wouldn't call her a shaman either.

She closed the ceremony with a final prayer and lit more candles, then gave us both a dry powdered mixture of tobacco, lime, honey and copal she called *San Pedro* and told Bodge to rub it on her stomach and arms and for me to do the same on my chest and arms "for the gripe." Then she said goodnight and left us. It was about 10pm, not even midnight, the ceremony having started at 5pm. This was odd. With the exception of San Pedro cactus ceremonies which sometimes take place in daylight, all teacher plants prefer darkness so ceremonies are mostly held at night, but I had never been to or heard of a night-time event which began or finished as early as Julia's.[26] Again, it felt like Julia had "lost it" – the magic, the power, the healing, the meaning – if she had ever had it, and that she just wanted an early close so she could go back to following the soap operas that she spent most of her days watching on her cranky television.

But maybe this was how all mushroom ceremonies were conducted in Huautla now? Maybe things had changed since Maria Sabina's day? Julia had a good reputation after all as a Thirteenth Grandmother. We decided we should give her the benefit of the doubt and attend another event.

In our next ceremony we were joined by Omar, her son, and two other people – Francisco and Ricardo, both Mexicans living just outside the town who were "very ill" according to Julia. The ceremony was different with locals present, much more interactive. The healers, Julia and Omar, were more involved and there was back-and-forth talking between shamans and patients, not reverential silence. Throughout the whole ritual the two newcomers had lots of questions for Omar, punctuated by grunts and sighs and moaning.

Even though I could hardly relax for the noise and disturbances, I was glad to have experienced this event. It gave credence to Maria Sabina's statement that Mexicans come to ceremonies for straightforward healing, whereas Westerners come to "find God" (whatever that means) and then put their curanderos on a ridiculous pedestal instead of interacting with them as people and, ironically, block their own healing as a consequence. The locals in this ceremony at least (who presumably know better than any New Age Westerner what a mushroom ceremony *should* be and how to behave at one) had no problems in relating to Julia as an equal and making their own needs known. As Elizabeth de la Portilla states: "A healer is a friend but not a friend, a guide and teacher but the honest ones tell their clients that the real work is taken on by the individual. Above all what I have learned from the healers is that faith and compassion are the real magic. To learn to heal myself is to practice the incredible."

Julia was content once again to sit in her cockpit all night and do even less than before as Omar took over some of the prayers and singing and did all of the healing in the form of *chupa*: the magical sucking from the body of the spiritual poisons, bad energies or "demons" that are causing the patient's sickness. At first he sat in the cockpit next to his mother, and asked out loud how Francisco and Ricardo were feeling at different points in the night. As they answered he sort of sucked the "bad air" from their words as they hung in the room, and from their breath that carried them then belched loudly to get rid of it. Later he went over and knelt next to them, sucking directly on their bodies and then spitting their disease out of the window. He prayed as he sucked, calling on support from the saints and demanding that the bad spirits leave "en el nombre de Jesus y Santa Maria, madre de dios."

Again, we were given an odd number of mushrooms (five and seven), not a pair as Wasson tells us is "always" the case, but Omar came round mid-ceremony to ask if we'd like more. I said yes and he handed me another three, so that's ten tonight and five yesterday with no real pattern to it and no logical progression either.

Omar closed the ceremony in the same way as the night before, with the "spiritual protection" of San Pedro which tonight he applied as small crosses or Xs to our palms, wrists, the insides of the elbows, the stomach, back and neck. He then cleansed us, as well as the room and the altar with copal incense and made final prayers to close the ceremony. By now it was 10pm. The ceremony had again taken five hours.

The next day I had questions for Julia. *Why does she never eat the mushrooms herself when running a ceremony?* Wasson's Maria Sabina did, as has every shaman of every plant tradition I've ever worked with; they all take their own medicine (even if the patient doesn't) in order for them to see the sickness and dis-ease they must heal. *Why does she not sing plant songs?* She is a plant healer, after all, and every other shaman in these traditions has made allies of the plants she works with and can call them into ceremony through song. Why doesn't she? *Why is she praying to the saints and not the plants as other shamans do? Why does she not perform healings? Why does she read from a Catholic hymn sheet instead of allowing the spirits to direct her?*

Julia didn't seem keen on talking though and waved me off so she could go back to watching another soap on her television, so I spoke to Omar instead who, it turned out, is her *grandson*, not her son, which makes her even older than I first thought.

He tells me that he has been training as a mushroom shaman for 15 years and has assisted his grandmother at events like these for ten. He tells me that he has eaten mushrooms for so long that "I don't need to eat them anymore to feel their energy." This, he suggests, is why Julia doesn't take them in ceremony either. I remain unconvinced as I know ayahuasceros in Peru who have drunk ayahuasca for 50 years but still take a cup at the start of every ceremony. Even if they do not "need" it in order to heal their patients they would consider it disrespectful to the spirit of the plant and impolite to their participants not to drink. "If I have a difficult patient or feel I need it I might eat one or two," Omar concedes. "But I always fast for two days before a ceremony – no food, no beer, no coffee" – though this does not seem to be a standard thing among the curanderos in his family either as just yesterday his grandmother was eating soup and meat for lunch a few hours before leading a ceremony.

"My job is to control the energy of the room and keep dark spirits out," he says. "I see them in people as shadows with no eyes or mouth. Then I sing and pray for light from the 'Big Spirit', and the patient should pray as well for light." This reminded me to ask why there were no songs for the plants, even the mushrooms, to call on them for assistance, but only to saints. According to Omar, however, even though I had listened closely and heard no plant songs in any of their ceremonies, I had this wrong. "We sing to the saints, the people *and* the plants," he said. "It is important to sing because that's the way the energy moves and prayers are communicated. That's the way it is done with all plants, whether mushrooms, iboga, peyote, ayahuasca ... The healing is in the words because words change things. Songs are a password to the world of God." Maria Sabina had said something similar – that healing *is* the word, the word and the breath. McKenna also, borrowing another of his original ideas from someone decades before him, maintained that "The syntactical nature of reality, the real secret of magic, is that the world is made of words. And if you know the words that the world is made of you can make of it whatever you wish."

Omar continued, "Yes the patient should certainly pray. They should take responsibility for themselves and their healing. They must take the ceremony seriously and be like they would in a church. Show respect to others and show respect to themselves." Again, I was reminded of a story about Maria Sabina and how she had been shocked and disgusted when one of the hippies in her ceremony started screaming during a trip and wanted her to save him. To Maria it seemed weak and undignified. Again, as Elizabeth de la Portilla, says, "the real work is taken on by the individual," i.e. by the patient himself. You do not over-extend yourself on mushrooms then go whining to someone else (especially a frail old lady) to rescue you. You take it like a man, learn from it, or you save yourself.

I was disappointed by Julia and the lack of power and spiritual authority in her ceremonies, but I couldn't say that she was fraudulent or that her rituals were out of keeping with the way that things are now done in Huautla, having only had ceremonies so far with her. Perhaps these days, since the flood of Wasson's hippies, all ceremonies are done for tourist dollars and only a watered-down version is offered, to outsiders at least. The only way to find out was to attend a ritual led by a different shaman and then compare the two. We asked around town for recommendations and one name kept coming up.

Ceremonies with Ines Cortes Rodriguez, student of Maria Sabina

She was, we were told, one of the last students of Maria Sabina. If that was true she must have begun her training young because she only looked in her late forties now. She says that from the age of five she knew what a mushroom ceremony was because her parents took her to them and at nine she tried mushrooms for the first time. She remembered Maria Sabina as a humble woman and a great healer, though always poor. She also remembered "those who cheated her" as well as the "characters who came from Europe," one of whom was John Lennon. "I was just a little girl when he came," she said. "I saw him. He walked into town in his high boots and his glasses with a guitar on his back. Then all the hippies turned up."

Inés is an example of the syncretic spiritual tradition which still exists in Huautla since she is a curandera – a witch, a *bruja,* a shaman – and also a Catholic. This is allowed, she says, because the church supports cures with mushrooms and many priests have also eaten and been cured by them. Like the Catholic Church in Huautla itself, Ines believes in many gods. "Just as there are many saints," she says, "there are many gods in the holy places. When I was 17 years old I almost died because I was enchanted in a nearby river." After that experience she became ill and felt that death was near. "Then my parents gave me ceremonies and I saw myself in the river with my hand up and half of my body in the water, I felt during the ceremony that I was going to die. That was already death. The next day I felt good and my parents told me to pay [the spirits for their healing, so] I brought cocoa, the red feather of the macaw and the egg of the turkey to the river."[27]

Her altar is not as big as Julia's, about 10 feet long, in the form of a table against the wall in her cellar, a small room of exposed brick, no windows, with two old mattresses laid out for us in front of it. Her altar is dedicated to a wider number of saints than Julia's. Their images are pinned to the wall and reach up to the ceiling. There are also candles, incense and fresh flowers.

We begin the ceremony with her at around 8pm at night, later than Julia begins hers and more in keeping with the arrangements of other shamans. Although we have been given no instructions on foods to avoid or diets to follow prior to the event, I normally fast for at least the day of the ceremony so I haven't eaten. This turns out to be fortuitous because I subsequently found a report online from someone who also attended a ceremony with Ines, which talked about "certain conditions that must be respected: the four days before [a ceremony] and the four following days it is forbidden to have sex and perform any kind of charity. The day of the ritual [food] should not be eaten, unless they are fruits, in order to avoid a heart-breaking bad stomach. 'Abstinence must be respected [or] you can go crazy. It's something sacred,' Inés had told us."[28]

First, she gives us a candle and a piece of copal to hold, then takes the copal and rubs it on our heads, chests, arms, legs, feet, finally making a cross with it on our foreheads before putting it into a burner. She does the same with the candles then places them on the altar. The copal is lit and the smoke blown around us, then the candles are lit. Already in this ceremony we have experienced more hands-on care and interaction than at any of Julia's events and, through this, there is a deepening into the sacred; the room starts to feel safe and holy.

She then gave us mushrooms – seven for me and five for Bodge, although, as the mushrooms were of different sizes, the net amount was probably the same for us both – but immediately apologized for them because, as she explained, it has rained so much recently that the mushrooms have lost some of their power. "Rain is very good for mushrooms but too much spoils them; they rot and lose *fuerza* [force]." While she spoke she chewed two mushrooms herself. Again, there were differences from Julia's ceremonies: the number of mushrooms was bigger (but still not in pairs, as Wasson insists), the fact that Ines ate them too, and her explanations and involvement with us as participants, as if we were of some importance or interest to her and not just a moneyed inconvenience. Then she began to teach us; Julia had hardly said a word to us in any of her events.

Four things are important for the ceremony:

Light: The light is the light of God. The big candle on the altar is the channel for God. It is where our prayers travel upwards and where God's love, will and healing travel down to us. The baby candles [the ones she had lit for us] are where God's light is born in the world through you.

Flowers: They are food for the saints. All the good spirits love beauty and beautiful smells which carry our prayers with them. The saints eat the essence of the flowers.

Copal: This is another beautiful smell and because I rubbed it on you it carries your essence so the spirits know you and your needs. It is also for purification and protection.

Cacao: This is for abundance. In the old days it was also used as money so the beans on the altar are your payments to the spirits for your healings.

As the mushrooms began to take effect she told us to lie down, then rubbed San Pedro on our foreheads, palms, wrists, elbows and stomachs. She also applied a drop of holy water to our heads, taken from a bottle on the altar shaped like the Virgen de Guadalupe.

About an hour into the ceremony, after many prayers and songs, some of them hymns but some of them original plant *tarjas*, she knelt down by us and began a *limpia* (cleansing) of our whole bodies with a bundle of leaves dipped in holy water, before resting it over our eyes as she prayed for our "cinco sentidos" [five senses] as well as our "hearts, minds, livers, lungs, digestive, circulatory and energy systems," and much more, naming every body part. Each prayer was personal, including our names, and precise, often beginning "Yo soy Ines Cortes. Vivo en Huautla, Oaxaca. Con mi eres Rocks Heaven y Bodge. Ven Guadalupe, ven ..." (I am Ines Cortes. I live in Huautla, Oaxaca. With me are Rocks Heaven [sic] and Bodge. Come Guadalupe, come), orations very similar in their personal nature to those which Maria Sabina used to make. She then sat back on her chair and began a long prayer of gratitude and blessings for the sacred healing plants and for the *hongos* (mushrooms). The saints she invoked were named for specific and purposeful reasons (for example, because I had told her that I worked with the teacher plant San Pedro, one of her prayers asked for the assistance of "San Pedro y San Pablo").

The ceremony ended in the early hours of the morning, about seven hours after it began. Ines gave us a cacao bean to eat then a glass of *Tres Coronas* wine from a bottle near her altar. Then she rubbed me with a piece of copal, asked me to kiss it, and then lit it, praying to the power and beauty of the light it made. From its flame – the way that it burned and the shapes it made – she performed a divination, giving me accurate information about my past and present life and the directions it might take in the future. To complete the healing she recommended that we take a *temezcal* (traditional sweatlodge sauna) to cleanse us. To me this felt like a real ceremony, unlike Julia's, where real work was undertaken by a real curandera, with results that could be felt.

Later, I found a blog account from someone who had also been healed by Ines, which demonstrated the consistencies in her approach as well as some of the differences which make her healings individual and meaningful:

> The holy children [mushrooms] were already on the table. Amadeo and I consumed fourteen each, and Carlos, more experienced, 16. Inés lit candles, incense, and began the ceremony with prayers in which she blessed us by naming us incessantly. [She cleansed us with] elder leaves ... Soon

I felt an abnormal weight on my body and I opted to go to bed. Thanks to fasting I did not have a bad stomach but I was cold, heavy and my mind was diffuse despite the attempts to concentrate. I had to close [my eyes] and a sinking feeling came. [Then] Inés appeared with her sacred songs. The same happened for three hours. When [my] mind was gone she reappeared praying and singing, reminding me that the goal was to control the journey towards a healing and not mere hallucination. From the cold I began to feel warm, I took off my jacket and began to sweat. The body was still slow and heavy, tense. I gritted my teeth, felt the floor swallow me. I looked around and saw Carlos and Amadeo reclining, all motionless. At some point I fell asleep.

"I felt that the earth was transmitting its energy," Carlos assures me the next day. Interested for many years in shamanism and tired of experimenting with drugs for recreational purposes, he chose to approach Ines seeking internal healing through the sacred plants. "Now, apart from continuing to experiment, the goal is a spiritual healing that leads me to know more, to love me. I'm looking to change the non-acceptance that I have, for the knowledge of my dark side and grow as a human being,"he stresses.

I ask Doña [a term of respect, like Doctor] Inés about the weight on the back that we all feel. She tells us that's why she gave us a [limpia, cleansing]: "That can [mean] damage or bad energies. And the heat that [you] felt later means healing, the expulsion of evil by sweat. The body brings a lot of humidity and the cold teaches you where the disease is. The heat is already healing, it draws out the toxins. When the body heals, the normal temperature returns. This is the work of the 'holy children' ... This is a sacred medicine. The 'holy children' make you wake up."[29]

Mushroom-eating Priests

We in the west have a firm division between institutionalised religion and spirituality (to the extent even that in some cases the soul is not regarded as a central part of religion. The practice of exorcism, for example – the casting out of bad energies and evil spirits, as Omar and Ines had done in their healings – is no longer continued in most religions and "possession" is seen as a sickness of the mind not the soul), but this is not the case in Huautla. Ines is being honest, for example, when she says that she is a devout Catholic even though she is also a "bruja" (witch) and "medicine woman," and accurate when she states that even Catholic priests come to ceremonies for healing from "the little children."

In an interview with Oliver Quintanilla, director of the documentary *Little Saints,* Father José Luis Sánchez, a Catholic priest from Huautla, agrees that "The mushroom rituals are part of a spirituality that can give great richness to the Church and the world." He continues:

> For the indigenous people God is both Father and Mother. In Europe God is only Father. That makes [the people] feel unease. [But] it's very elementary; we even find it at the beginning of the Bible, the duality of God. God the Father and Mother, the masculine and the feminine in God. [But] in Europe it still doesn't sound good to them. Because of their macho culture they still can't accept the concept of God Mother ...The Mazatecs have that ability [and in their ritual they also] invoke the owners of the hills, the *chicones*, the supernatural beings... along with the Christian saints ... Under the effect of the mushroom the Mazatecs dialogue with God, dialogue with the Saints, dialogue with Jesus Christ, with Mary, to find the light ...

"The Wise Ones who usually do not speak Spanish," he remarks

– meaning the curanderos and shamans who are part of a long traditional lineage and only speak the pure native languages – "use only a few elements of the Church. Their dialogue is with their supernatural beings." Yet even their rituals are still about achieving an encounter with some kind of God. They call the climax of their rite "reaching the sacred table": "to arrive [at] the table of riches ... where God will hand out his gifts, where God will give you the true light, where he will show you your path." Reaching this table, this state of grace, this pure mushroom intoxication where ego dissolves and unity is found, can be difficult for some and it is at such times that true healers excel, assisting their patients through words, songs and actions to push on and find God, grace, self, "cosmic consciousness"... or whatever else we want to call this state of divine healing and profound understanding.

> A truly Wise One never abandons their patient halfway through the trip. He or she will accompany the person throughout the journey ...
>
> Until the healer brings their patient back from where he or she went the rite is [not] completed. When people get lost – because sometimes we can find very beautiful things, it looks very nice –the sage, the true sage tells you, "Wait, you didn't come to see flowers, you didn't come to see colors, you didn't come to sing. What did you come for? What do you want to resolve? Well, look for it. Do not stay here in the beauty. Find your problem, solve it."
>
> When darkness or difficult things or animals or problems present, the wise one says, "Well this is your challenge. Follow it, follow it. You're going to win. Pray, ask God." And the wise one prays and starts to sing, uses *pisiete* [the San Pedro mixture of tobacco leaf mixed with lime], uses what the moment dictates. There isn't a structured liturgy, but the wise one reads *the now*, to figure out what he must do in order

to help overcome the problems. It's really a walk with the person you're serving.[30]

How to Be Part of a Safe and Effective Ritual (and How Not to)

While we were in Huautla we of course visited the home of Maria Sabina, nowadays a small rusty shack trying to be a basic shop with about half a dozen products for sale, run by one of her relatives. He immediately tried to talk us into an expensive ceremony to be led by Maria's "grandson" or "cousin"; the details were fluid.

We had been warned by the people of Huautla about Sabina's relatives who were, they said, defiling her memory and hoodwinking the dwindling tourist trade by trying to cash in on her fame. Like vultures round a corpse. It was tempting to give in to curiosity and join a ceremony, no matter how bad, just to sit in the room where history had been made but in the end it all seemed too seedy and shabby so we declined and walked back to our hotel in the ever-present rain, along the road that Lennon and Dylan walked in a time when things were different.

Huautla these days has fallen to the Yankee dollar. Our experiences with Julia and Maria Sabina's grandson/cousin made that obvious. Which begs the question, how do you know whether you are part of a genuine ceremony run by a skilled shaman who offers his services with good intention, or being drawn in by a con man, especially if you have little experience? The real answer is instinct; how do you feel in your heart and your gut when think about or talk to the shaman you are considering? To guide you in this there is a sort of mental checklist you can refer to, or a series of questions to ask yourself.

1. While no shaman will (or should be expected to) work for free (would you?), it is important to get a good feeling about who he's working *for* – you or Benjamin Franklin –

and a sense that he can really do the job, giving you not only value for money but more importantly, guidance, support and protection during the ceremony. It is hard to gauge this before attending at least one event with a shaman because at this point you have no reference for what represents value. For instance, I have had a few people tell me that, on paper, my ceremonies and trips overseas to work with indigenous shamans look expensive because before they attend one they are, of course, concerned only with *price*. After they have been in ceremony and the plants have worked their magic, healing them of serious illnesses or bringing them new insights and wisdom, they can understand *value* and then they tell me they would have paid ten times the price had they just *known* what they would receive. When we were speaking with Maria Sabina's relative, though, all he seemed to want to talk about was money. *This is the price. Is that too much? Ten percent off for you because you look like nice gringos. Half price if you bring the money by 2pm. How many ceremonies do you want? When can you bring the money?* At no point did he ask the more important and relevant questions: *What do you wish to get from your ceremony? Is there a particular issue or illness I can help you with?*

2. Does he explain the ceremony, the protocols, the effects of the mushrooms, etc., as part of a thorough briefing before the event begins so you are at ease and know what to do and expect? It may be possible to attend a ceremony to observe, without taking mushrooms, if you want to put your mind more at ease. Some shamans may not allow this but it's worth asking. Be prepared to pay for your place, however, whether you are taking mushrooms or not – which is fair because the shaman could otherwise have sold your space to somebody else if you weren't there so why should you get it for free?

3. Does he ensure that the room is safe, spiritually clean and protected? Some shamans perform a short ritual to "seal the room" before ceremony begins and, at the very least, there should be a cleansing of the room and its occupants. Even Julia gets a tick for performing a limpia.
4. During the event, does the shaman appear to be working on your behalf? It is not enough that he "has presence" or seems powerful; is he using this presence and power to benefit *you*? Does he make sure, for example, that everyone gets equal attention and (unless there are good reasons otherwise) an equal measure of mushrooms (at least three grams as less than that will not take you very far)?
5. Does he have original prayers, plant songs and chants of power based on diets he has undertaken and first-hand knowledge of the plants and their spirits – or is he reading from a song sheet by torchlight?
6. Is he *active* during the ceremony? Is there hands-on healing via *chupa, limpia,* the use of agua florida (flower water), the rattle, cleansing with tobacco etc., or does he remain seated all night leaving you to struggle alone?

The answers to these and other questions will make it clear to you whether or not you want to work with this healer. On top of this there are a few things you can do for yourself (or take care of for others if you are leading the ceremony) to ensure that you have a good and safe event. Basically it amounts to controlling *set* and *setting,* to use the terms invented by Leary during his mushroom research.

Set refers to the state of mind with which you approach your encounter with a teacher plant. Personally, I do not believe it is possible to have a "bad trip" with any entheogen, in the sense that there is anything contained within the plant itself which is deliberately out to show us disturbing images. All entheogens are there to teach and heal and as part of that process they may show us things that we have repressed and would prefer not to see, but these things are already within us and part of our sickness; they are not visions which the plant has imposed on us from elsewhere. The point of showing them to us is so that they can be known, brought to consciousness and dealt with, and their energy can be released since, hidden or not, these things are driving us in ways that we cannot predict or control. It is only when we become aware of them that we can hope to exercise freewill over our fate. The most important practice for avoiding difficulties during your journey or finding yourself unexpectedly face-to-face with these parts of your deep unconscious is to set an intention for your journey.

Intention provides a road map and a framework for the trip you are about to take. It gives it direction and purpose. Going into a journey without intention means a greater risk of chaos and of ending up overwhelmed, panicked and confused. Having a *reason* for taking the journey, however, means that everything you see, hear or feel relates to something definite. It may still be intense at times but in the context of your intention even chaos may be meaningful.

Fasting prior to the ceremony also helps focus the mind and aids intention. I find it best to forego all food on the day of the ceremony and take no liquids from about two hours before the event begins. Fasting also shows a commitment to the spirit of the mushrooms and says that you are serious about the work; something which the plant will reward you for. If you really can't face a fast, however, then at least undertake a short shamanic diet. As we saw in Huautla different shamans mean different things by "diet" but there are taboo items on practically every shamanic diet – alcohol, pork, lemons, salt, spices, sex – and these, at least, should be avoided altogether on the day of the ceremony and, preferably, the days before and after it.

Setting refers to the environment and circumstances in which mushrooms are taken. In all shamanic work, ritual precautions are essential since you will be dealing with spirits and energies which are otherwise uncontained. The results of this can be unpredictable at best, so always ensure that mushrooms are taken in a safe, calm, quiet space, in darkness, away from people who are not taking part in the ceremony, and away from noise and distractions. This is basic common sense and spiritual etiquette. In most ceremonies, Julia's aside, excessive noise, giggling and talking, as well as unnecessary movements, are also frowned upon as they distract everyone from their spiritual journey.

The foregoing should be considered the *basic* precautions for working with mushrooms in any ceremonial situation. If you wish to work shamanically with the plant, however, you will also want to introduce a more formal ritual aspect. This will help you create a bond with the spirits of the mushrooms, alert them to your intention, and give you a useful psychological boundary to assist your work and enhance your safety by providing the session with a definite beginning and end.

My own procedure is firstly to create a safe container by making prayers to the saints, to the spirits of the mushrooms and to the other helpful spirits I wish to watch over the ceremony, and then to the seven directions of east, south, west, north, above (Heaven, the sky), below (the Earth) and the center where, symbolically, we sit, so we are protected on all sides. I then seal this sacred space with a rattle, agua florida and tobacco smoke to keep it pure. Following that, I make a prayer and light a candle before a statue of the Virgin which sits at the back of the room watching over all participants.

Once this is done I hand each person a plate containing mushrooms, cacao beans and a glass of tequila. We eat and drink in silence (I always eat too), and people are encouraged not to speak or move during the night so as not to disturb others or, indeed, their own process with the teacher plant.

My ceremonies normally start at around 8pm and last for some hours until we cross the symbolic threshold of midnight and enter a new day together. I sit with a *mesa* (a small cloth altar on which are laid shamanic healing tools like rattles and crystals that are useful or necessary during ceremony) and welcome the mushroom spirits and the saints with prayers, invocations, *oraciones* and *cantos* – songs similar to the *icaros* used by ayahuasca shamans to summon and transmit to participants the healing powers of the plants they have dieted, the saints that are their allies and the power objects on their mesas. Maria Sabina began with a slightly different ritual, by introducing herself to the spirits and enlisting their support. As Wasson tells us, "Chanting early in the night, Eva Mendez lists her qualifications: 'Am I not good? I am a creator woman, a star woman, a moon woman, a cross woman, a woman of heaven. I am a cloud person, a dew-on-the-grass person'."[31] Whatever the approach, this signals the start of the ceremony and puts everyone present on notice.

At some point during the night it is likely that I will move around the room to conduct a healing for each person present, as well as making prayers before the altar for the good of the ceremony in general and for those who are absent but in need of love and healing. At the very end I close the ceremony by offering a prayer of thanks to the spirits who have watched over us, and releasing them from our ceremony. This does not necessarily mean that the mushrooms have lost all power, however, and some people may remain in their effect for several more hours, but there will be no more singing or prayer as the journey is now a personal one of healing and self-discovery.

Nobody – no human being, that is – showed me how to make a ceremony like this; it is a process that developed over years of practice through inspiration from spirit. This is the best approach with any ceremony since all rituals gain power when they are personalised so that you invest yourself in them. The key things are these: that on the part of the healer there should always be reverence for and deference to the plant which is the real healer in these events, always a pure intention to help and to heal and, as much as possible, you should try to get yourself out of the way so that you as the shaman become a channel, a "hollow bone" through which the spirits pass to conduct their healings.

To illustrate what can go wrong when these principles are ignored, I want to tell you about a ceremony in New Zealand which has now become a legendary "How Not To" event. It was organized by Jennifer Howell, a self-styled "traditional shaman" (even though she is an immigrant from Texas with no Maori lineage) who ran the Sacred Balance healing center in Hamilton (now in Ostend on Waiheke Island).

Her first mistake was a lack of focus, having booked a teacher to lead a training course for a week on land belonging to her father, but getting the dates wrong so that at the end of the workshop they were left with a day to fill. She decided, more-or-less on a whim, to fill it with a plant ceremony. This was her second mistake: a complete lack of preparation to work with these powerful plants. Her third was a lack of respect for their spirits, expecting them to just show up and do what she told them to in order to cover her error. There were a number of other problems too:

1. She had been allowing her students to party in her hot tub after class all week, drinking and smoking cannabis, so there had been no proper diet followed.
2. She had made no checks with participants to understand their medical history or any problems or needs they might have.
3. She had no experience of leading ceremonies, though she had attended a few.
4. The event would run on her father's land, without his knowledge or permission, so she was also involving him, without his awareness, in what the authorities would regard as an illegal activity using a Class A drug.

The scene was set for disaster and that's exactly what she got when during her ceremony one woman had a serious psychotic breakdown which would go on to last for almost a week. Had Jenn bothered to check in advance she would have discovered that this participant had a history of psychological problems brought on by the use of cannabis, which she had been allowed to smoke all week, and had spent time in a mental hospital due to a previous breakdown.

As the ceremony went on, Jenn showed herself to be completely out of her depth and added to the problem with her own hysteria, making it necessary for her teacher to step in and handle the sick woman. As soon as the ceremony ended Jenn wanted the woman off her property so she did not draw the attention of her father who lived nearby. Her "solution" was to fob the woman off on another unqualified friend who lived in town and, when that didn't work, she suggested that the woman be abandoned to wander the streets in the middle of a continuing psychosis. She said she didn't much care if the woman died as long as it was not traceable to her as she was afraid that her children would be taken off her if the authorities discovered what she had done.

Again her teacher stepped in and took over, spending four days with the woman 24/7 to nurse her back to a reasonable state of health, then arranging for a relative to fly from Australia to collect her. As an expression of her gratitude, in order to distance herself from the disaster she had been part of, Jenn refused to pay her teacher for the work he had done and began to spread rumors that he had sexually abused the sick girl, even though the "victim" herself flat out denied it. Her final act of arse-covering was to sack her assistant who had helped deal with the problem all week while Jenn herself had done nothing of practical use.

There is a happy ending to this story as the sick girl eventually recovered but it could easily have ended differently except for the charity of others – even in death and arrests. These problems could also have been easily avoided by showing respect to the plants and following the principles of a good ceremony.

3

The Effects and Healing of Mushrooms

Psychedelics are a very rapid way to induce very meaningful change in people.

Dr Albert Garcia-Romeu, Johns Hopkins University

Jenn's behavior (in the last chapter) was shameful and she was, rightly, cast out by her teacher. But the sick woman was not entirely innocent either since she of course knew her own history of mental illness, she knew that cannabis was a trigger and she was not being forced to smoke the joints that were on offer at Jenn's. Once again, ultimately it is we who are responsible for our own well-being, our safety, our healing, ourselves; nobody else.

Taking responsibility begins with research, knowledge and awareness so we understand what to expect from a mushroom trip and from the ceremony. We have already looked at the nature of ceremonies, good and bad, and the important principles to follow when attending or leading one, so this chapter looks at the effects of magic mushrooms and the healing that is possible from them.

Effects

There are nearly 200 species of magic mushroom within the family *Strophariaceae*, all of which contain psilocybin (O-phosphoryl-4-hydroxy-N,N-dimethyltryptamine) and psilocin (4-hydroxy-N,N-dimethyltryptamine). Psilocybin, the better known of these chemicals, is metabolized after ingestion into psilocin, which is actually the primary active chemical.

The effects of these mushrooms are subjective and vary considerably by species as well as among individual users.

Factors include time of picking, whether fresh or dried, body weight of the user, the user's experience and tolerance, and so on. Mind-altering effects may last up to eight hours with decreasing intensity over time, the first three to four hours being the peak, during which the user experiences the most vivid visuals and distortions of commonly accepted reality. The effects can seem to last much longer to the user, however, as psilocybin also alters the perception of time.

Noticeable changes to the auditory, visual, and tactile senses usually become apparent around 30 minutes to an hour after ingestion, but can come on more quickly (after five or ten minutes in some cases, or even almost immediately after consumption), with 30–40 minutes being a good average. Visual shifts include enhancement and contrasting of colors, auras or halos seen around lights, increased visual acuity, surfaces that ripple, shimmer or breathe, complex open and closed eye visuals, and objects that warp or morph. Sounds may be heard with increased clarity. Distant noises can seem close, for example. Music can take on a more profound sense of cadence and depth; and tiny sounds (such as a mosquito in the room) can seem extremely loud and to grow louder as we give more conscious attention to them. Some users also experience synaesthesia, where the senses become mixed, so that a color or taste produces a particular sound, for example.

Letcher[32] puts all of this a bit more poetically:

> Normal vision is disrupted by juddering fractal textures and patterns that emerge out of, and are superimposed upon, the apparent world. Everything is suddenly tattooed with light, while unbidden faces may peer out from the woodwork ... The epithet "magic" appears apposite and well-earned for mushrooms create an overall ambience of earthy, Tolkeinesque enchantment.
>
> The world, and especially the natural world, appears in a

> new light, as if some ordinarily obscured and secret aspect of it has been suddenly revealed. The smallest details ... appear exquisitely beautiful and heavy with meaning. Consciousness appears less bounded than it is ordinarily, for trees, plants and rocks seem to be, in some peculiar sense, aware ... [H] owever strange and unsettling this transformation, the bemushroomed may report a feeling of familiarity, of déjà vu, of having always known about this particular nook in the architecture of experience. Some say it is as if they have stepped into an archetypal space ... a place where things of great importance will be revealed. These are the shamanic realms, myconauts claim, where autonomous, discarnate beings, the spirits of shamanism, impart information and reveal gnostic truths. Some report hearing the "mushroom" talking to them, as clear as day.

These senses, feelings and visuals can be accompanied by the resurfacing of sometimes forgotten memories, usually with emotional depth. There are other changes too, including a sense of warmth (or sometimes cold) and of melting into the environment. Feelings (good or bad) are amplified and made more intense. The user is often left with a sense of awe at the power of the mushroom, the beauty (sadness, glory, tragedy ...) of the world, and/or wonder at themselves and their surroundings.

Whatever dramatic, shattering, explosive or enlightening effects the mushrooms may have, however, there is normally nothing hurtful and no lasting damage from the experience. A study by Professor David Nutt, a former chief drugs adviser to the British government, published by the *Lancet* journal found that mushrooms caused the least harm to self or others of 20 drugs examined, including alcohol, tobacco, heroin and cocaine. Alcohol was found to be the most harmful drug, scoring 72 out of a possible 100, far more damaging than heroin (55) or crack cocaine (54). Mushrooms ranked lowest of all in terms of harm, with a score of less than 10 points compared, for example, with meth (34), tobacco (27) and speed (amphetamines) (22).

In their book *TIHKAL* (Tryptamines I Have Known and Loved) Alexander and Ann Shulgin outline the effects of psilocybin at various doses. Bear in mind that these are personal observations, not all of which will be relevant to you, and also that in ceremony you are unlikely to be given the lower dose levels described here, an effective ceremonial dose being around three grams minimum.

- 6.6 mg: "Something has started … some hints of animal faces [visions or hallucinations] … No movement, nothing flows, but it probably wouldn't take much effort. Another hour and I am dropping off [coming down] already ..."
- 7 mg: "Basically I am not in a pleasant place – quite neurotic –inwardly turned –a touch of despair – considerable visual activity and if I were with someone I might find some sort of reinforcement. The apathy and unpleasantness is ebbing now. My mood might have been negative and the psilocybin simply amplified everything. There was some intensification of the lights and darks around me."
- 10 mg: "Approximately forty minutes after the start, there was a flutter and a very high, stimulated feeling, and gradually things began to move very rapidly. It was astounding. When I closed my eyes I saw so many fantastically beautiful patterns, textures, colors. Everywhere I looked, eyes open, the colors were brilliant. The house looked absolutely gorgeous and nature was simply spectacular. It was a little frightening, almost too exciting, after the gentleness of other substances. I could not believe that I was doing it, and that I had the power within myself to see such beauty. I don't know how long this went on but the motion was so rapid that I felt a sort of motion sickness. Then I became quite nauseated

and remained nauseated the rest of the day, until things quieted down in the evening, and then I felt absolutely wonderful."

- 15 mg: "Visual distortions. Things distract me. I can't find the cap to my pen – must I keep writing forever? At this point I couldn't drive, let alone write, and it is just a bit more than a half hour since I took it. The furniture in my office is moving up and down. I lie down and close my eyes. THIS is where it is at. Visuals are wild. Even with eyes open, with no visual target, there are imaginative visual effects. I imagine a dark room with a fireplace going in the middle of the night, with no other inputs and with my eyes closed I have the body image of being seated in front of that fire and I am amazed by the hallucinations and distortions I am seeing there, only there is no fireplace as I am still lying in my darkened bedroom. Sort of a 2x removed hallucination. This is a night-time drug – the day-light washes everything out. I tried but could not repeat the fireplace thing and must be dropping rapidly."
- 1.5 g [possible low ceremonial dose]: "Speckled patterning with my eyes closed, and in general a light intoxication. Certainly not the sparkle of LSD. Dropped quickly and felt heavy and tired, good sleep."
- 3.5 g [possible average ceremonial dose]: "Everything was coming at me in waves, boxing me in, the visuals were in waves and in dark earth colors, orange and brown, not the wide spectrum of acid. I was sea-sick, and vomiting helps some, and a little dope quieted the tummy. Started dropping, and everything became very good, and by midnight I was out. No hangover at all."

Some notes on Shulgin's accounts. Firstly, he seems to have a peculiar relationship to psilocybin as he is effected at extremely low doses but feels less effect (or is made ill) from a relatively normal dose. This is unusual. It is also, by the way, rare for anyone to vomit as a result of eating mushrooms. I have never seen it. Secondly, never, please, mix plants in the way Shulgin describes in his 3.5g account – mushrooms and "a little dope." It is extremely disrespectful to the plants themselves and may also cause problems for you. Remember what happened to Jenn's student when she did the same.

The foregoing are rather cold, clinical observations and, as I said, some of them by no means apply to everyone. More typical encounters with the spirit of the mushrooms, the mood evoked and the healing and learning associated with them can be found in the examples that follow. The first is from the website Erowid (www.erowid.org), where you'll also find others, which the author calls his *Woodland Initiation*.

> After about 45–50 minutes I heard a "voice" calling to me. It wasn't audible in the normal sense – it came from inside my own mind! It was a woman! "Yooo-hooo Cameron! Come on Cameron – it's time," she beckoned ... Then I was GONE – out of this world. I escaped into what I perceived to be the outer boundaries of my mind or my imagination. This presented itself as a natural forest with low light. Here I met the owner of the aforementioned voice – the Mushroom Goddess. She took the form of a white, strapless, ankle-length dress, standing side-on from me. For about the next two hours I dialogued with her, becoming totally bewitched by her charm, her wit, her intelligence, her knowledge, her unconditional affection for me and her seemingly infinite perspective.
>
> This dialogue took the form of telepathy and explained in part the relationship between mushrooms and human beings: "she had formed symbiotic relationships with animals [and humans] and taken them on an evolutionary journey."
>
> I was shown futuristic cities, some of them suspended

> in space!! But I was not shown any of their inhabitants. The journey in this dimension continued for about 3 hours, after which time I was deposited back into my mind, into my body and into my reality as though nothing had happened, apart from the fact that I was very deeply impressed. At no time did I feel any anxiety...
>
> Since that time, the question which begs most in my mind about my experience is "What did I ever DO to deserve such a miraculous thing?" The only answer I can find is that this was my reward for seeking truth so passionately, never being satisfied to allow religion, the establishment, the mass media, science or even myself to define truth for me. A reward for my scepticism maybe. Despite my speculations about my initiation, I DO know that it is the definitive point of my life. Something of another rebirth, and something which has restored my hope for the future and the continued survival of our species.

Here is another story by one of my students, which is quite similar to the one above. Shamans, of course, maintain that teacher plants like mushrooms have their own consciousness, sentience, landscape and *spirit*, and both of these accounts – not by shamans but by novices – appear to confirm this.

> I was an eighteen year old hippie at the time and had absolutely no knowledge of shamanism. I had taken LSD and liberty cap mushrooms a few times and had the usual tripping effects such as insights into things, lots of laughing at the absurdity of it all, some paranoia, a love of the natural world and certain revelations such as being a microcosm of the microcosm but as regards meeting entities, spirits or indeed anything beyond the contents of my own head ... no.
>
> The Mull of Kintyre is a truly magical place. The light

changes constantly on the hills and over the waters to Arran. It was September 1975 and I was on holiday on the Skipness estate. I used to fish with a fly for sea trout on the little Clonaig river when it was in spate. One day fishing I realized the field by the little bridge on the Clonaig river was covered with psilocybin mushrooms. It was too good an opportunity to miss so putting down my tackle I picked several hundred in a short space of time. I walked back to Skipness along the old drover's road in the hills and there were mushrooms everywhere. Over the next few days avoiding the eye of the gamekeeper I picked a few thousand mushrooms and dried them in the airing cupboard with the intention of putting them through a coffee grinder and making mushroom honey. On the Saturday night my girlfriend was going out to West Loch Tarbert for a girls' night out at the pub so I decided to take a large dose of mushrooms to see what happened. I took a hundred fresh liberty caps from the basket I had picked, put them in a teapot poured some boiling water over them and left them to brew. After allowing the brew to cool I drank all the tea and went upstairs to lie on my bed and wait for the effects to come on.

I do not remember exactly what was going on in my life at that time but there were problems that needed addressing and I was used to occasionally using psychedelics to work through stuff and make decisions. After some time I felt slightly nauseous. I was aware that 100 was a huge dose but I had little fear as I knew they were not poisonous.

Then suddenly I became aware of the most beautiful song so far far away as if in another corner of the universe. It was incredibly faint but I could just hear it. My attention was gripped. What on earth is this? Then I realized it was coming towards me singing, singing and that it was not in any language I had ever heard. I remember its rolling joyful pitch and I was not frightened but curious. My goodness it is coming for me I thought. The song became louder and louder and suddenly – ping! – I was in the presence of what I could only describe as the God of the mushrooms. His song seemed to be rolling over and over across eons of time. I was aware that he was unlike any life form I had ever come across or imagined and he was not part of the contents of my own psyche. I was filled with a sense of awe. Our minds connected telepathically and I think (it was forty two years ago) he asked me what I wanted. I cannot exactly remember what went down except I was given a lesson pertinent to my life at that time. That was it ... I was given a lesson.

We spoke telepathically. Our minds were joined. My problems and how to proceed in my life were addressed and I knew what I should do. As soon as the lesson was over I became aware that the visitation was over and he started his singing again and with great power and beauty he started moving away from me farther and farther away until his song began to fade into the distance. It was a rolling song, rolling over and over slowly disappearing into the night growing moment by moment further and further away. Then he was gone and I was lying on my bed and stretching out my body. There was a candle lit on the chest of drawers and it was now raining outside. I started to come out of the experience a little and lay listening to the night and the soothing sound of rain falling. I had a great sense of peace somehow integrated with awe and wonder. I had met the God of the mushrooms. This was really amazing ...

After a while I heard a car crunching the gravel driveway and Sarah was back from the pub. I ran downstairs to greet a mildly tipsy Sarah. I have just met the God of the mushrooms I blurted out.

I have never forgotten this and it wasn't until around thirty years later when I attended an ayahusaca ceremony that I put two and two together ... I really *had* met the God of the

> mushrooms. Perhaps our forebears before Christianity had the knowledge of how to work with the God of the mushrooms for healing and for divination I rather think they did. It's really good to share this story as it's been puzzling me for years. What I learned from this was that there *is* a spirit of the mushrooms. My first impression was that it was a God as that was how I described him to Sarah. I use the masculine here as the energy did not seem feminine whereas the ayahuasca seemed feminine. The spirit of the mushrooms can act as a teacher, protector guide and healer. As to the nature, origin and life of the spirit, it is a mystery [but it seemed to me] that there is a huge similarity between the ayahuasca experience and the psilocybin mushroom experience. Ingesting the mushrooms opens a doorway to the spiritual world.

Here is an account from another student who, on their first use of mushrooms (in a context I definitely do not recommend to you, by the way), met with a loving, wise and protective being which may have been the spirit of the plant:

> Sixteen years of age – that was my first time with mushrooms. Having no idea what they were or what they would do to me, the thinking, which I now know as right-brained, told me that it was from earth and wouldn't harm me. Of course that is not always true, but somewhere in the fog of being lost in hormones and unfortunate human experiences, I knew it was right. I ate them out of the bag without reservation. Then, I immediately got in my car, a 1964 Ford Falcon Futura that I still miss to this day. Being a teenager in the '80s was more free than it is today. We could explore our surroundings and ourselves without cameras on us at all times. Rule-breaking was easy. So I thought nothing of getting in my car to drive home by myself after just ingesting something that I had little idea about and no idea of what would or could happen.

Within about 20 minutes of driving, a person appeared in the seat next to me. It was night time and I lived in a rural place with those small, dark country roads that nobody travels on, especially late at night. I do not remember even one car coming or going. Every time I stopped the car to look at the figure next to me straight-on instead of peripherally, it disappeared. It didn't scare me although it was my first introduction to the opening of the mind through plants and I was by myself.

This being was without true human form, but took a form that I could accept and that looked human-*like* and it did nothing but sit next to me in my car as I drove. Soon the little white dashed line in the middle of the road started to jump off the road, with each white dash becoming a snake and they put on a show, trading off wiggling to the left, then the right, left then the right. Then they would jump instead of wiggle – left and right, alternating in an organized way. When I started to concentrate too hard on the dashed line, my "phantom person" would appear again, focusing me on the task of driving. I distinctly remember that driving my car became automatic – almost as if I was not really driving at all. The non-person-person just sat next to me as if we were on our way to a picnic in the middle of the night. But here's the thing about the dashed white line in the middle of the road: they were never there. That part of the country is so rural that only recently (in the 2000s) have lines been painted on the road. They were never there in the 1980s when this happened. Maybe they were sent by the mushrooms to see me home safely. I don't try to second guess it.

That is where the memory stops except I know there must have been a lot more to it. I have taken mushrooms about a half-dozen times since then with various friends in various settings. What I know most about mushrooms is love, and being able to feel it on that cellular level. But really what I appreciate most about mushrooms is the mystery and being able to live in that mystery in a true and wild way. That experience planted a seed of confidence inside me that feeds me to this day. That being was sent to protect me and to give me a certain confidence that few people get to experience.

To my 16-year-old brain it was just an experience and I'm not sure I recognized the significance of it until recently, after coming back to plant medicines to re-open my mind. Think of all of the experiences you can have in 36 years. That mushroom-filled night was one that did not fade even a little. I can still recall the person sitting next to me in my car as if it were yesterday. Make of that what you will.

These encounters with a single entity that seems to be the spirit of the mushrooms are rare, by the way, so don't let them set up an expectation for your own ceremonies. It is true that the mushroom "plant" in its entirety is one of the biggest single organisms on Earth, the mushroom itself being only a tiny part of the whole, as Letcher points out, "for it is merely the reproductive structure or fruiting body ... The main body actually consists of a network of microscopic threads or hyphae which grow and branch through the species' preferred substrate, forming what is called a mycelium. Mycelia can grow to a vast size. One of the largest has been found in America, a single root fungus, *Armillaria bulbosa*. This specimen occupies an area of about fifteen hectares, weighs in the region of 10,000kg, and is probably about fifteen hundred years old." So, as a single, cohesive and gigantic entity we might expect mushrooms to have a single, cohesive and gigantic spirit to match, but this is typically not what shamans find. Although some in Mexico relate the "mushroom spirit" to the Virgen de Guadalupe (by which the curanderos of Mexico more likely mean *Tonantzin* – also known as *Chālchiuhcihuātl*: Emerald/Jade Woman – the Earth goddess, rather than the Catholicized "mother of Christ" version)[33] they more generally refer to the mushrooms as "the holy children" or "the little saints," in the plural, implying that the energy field or mushroom "entity" contains multiple aspects or consciousnesses. These multiple aspects are the mushrooms themselves, as if each one has its own identity while also being a part of the collective (mycelium). During mushroom intoxication these individual spirits are sometimes described as looking like "tiny blue lights," or "imps" or "giggling, mischievous children."

Healing Encounters

Sometimes mushroom trips (or some parts of a trip anyway) are apparently quite straightforward and they can certainly be more direct when they are taken for healing rather than transcendental motives. Erica Rex described her experience for the *Independent* newspaper.[34]

> I was diagnosed with breast cancer in 2009. A year on from a lumpectomy and radiation therapy, now on aromatase inhibitors, my prognosis seemed good. But rather than cheerfully getting on with life, I was spending most days at my desk crying. I began searching the web for a way to kill myself that wouldn't be either messy or too painful. Both here in the UK and in the US, where I had my surgery, medicine excels at finding cures for disease and saving lives. All that excellence has created a kind of void, wherein treatment of the disease has trumped the human needs of those being treated. My demoralisation is common among cancer patients. We obsess about survival and what the future holds for us.

Because of her condition Erica volunteered to take part in a study by the Johns Hopkins School of Medicine to see whether psilocybin can help cancer patients regain a sense of meaning in the face of their disease and alleviate the anxiety and depression associated with cancer.

When my session day arrived, I was brought into a softly lit, comfortably decorated lounge, invited to lie down on a sofa and listen to music. Then I swallowed a purple capsule of psilocybin. Some time later, when I was deeply within the world of the drug and the imagery it evoked, I found myself inside a steel industrial space. I became aware of my animosity towards my two living siblings. A woman sitting at the end of a long table, wearing a net cap, white clothes, and working busily, turned and handed me a Dixie cup. "You can put that in here," she said. So I did. The cup filled itself with my bilious, sibling-directed feelings. "We'll put it over here," she said, and placed it on a table at the back of the room. Then she went matter-of-factly back to work, along with now-numerous busy women. At that point, my guide Fred asked me what was happening. I recounted the scene and then I began to laugh out loud. My own laughter appeared to me in a midnight-blue, cloud-dark sky as an effusion of twinkling gemstones. I was in two places at once, both in the session room, talking to my guide, and in the other world of the drug, with its own aesthetics and its own logic.

Not all subjects have an all-encompassing transcendent experience during their sessions, wherein they feel a profound oneness of all things, a union with the Universe or with God. I did not – and was at first disappointed. But as the months have passed, I realize what I did gain is immeasurable. Since my session, my mood has improved, and my sense of myself, as a person occupying a certain space in the Universe, has altered. Later on, when talking about my hallucinations with the clinicians and my guides, I found they provided me with some profound truths about my life, my feelings and my sense of myself. My tendency to judge myself with a kind of murderous harshness has ebbed. I'm now able to feel more compassion towards myself. I no longer spend days worrying about the future, and about whether I'll have

> a cancer recurrence, or whether I'll die alone ... The drug is a skeleton key which unlocks an interior door to places we don't generally have access to ... It's a therapeutic accelerant.

Nick W has a similar story of healing.[35]

> Growing up in a home with alcohol abuse had quite an impact on me. As a child I saw the demons my father struggled with on nearly a daily basis. I watched as alcoholism slowly turned my loving, caring and compassionate father into a monster to be feared. His rage was terrifying ... Throughout my childhood I always felt alone. I was often bullied in school and had very few friends. Both at school and at home I learned [to] stay out of the way. I learned that I couldn't trust others, even the ones I loved. I learned failure, humiliation, rejection, worthlessness, and disgrace.
>
> I started drinking in high school. Drinking allowed me, for the very first time, to feel normal. It took away the insecurities, the shame, guilt and the way I thought about myself. I felt energy, I felt control, and for that fleeting moment the void inside me disappeared. For me it was the only way I knew how to cope and I soon developed a habit of self-medicating four nights a week. After I graduated high school and continued into college my habits progressed. Not only did my drinking continue but I learned to fill the void in other ways. I used women and sex ... I smoked cigarettes, slept very little and had obsessive and compulsive tendencies.
>
> My breaking point came shortly after college ended and an emotionally abusive relationship sent me spiralling into a psychological breakdown. Unknown at the time, the relationship triggered a lot of past emotional issues buried deep within my psyche. What followed were months of a debilitating depression and thoughts of suicide. After experiencing multiple anxiety attacks, I learned that I suffered

from complex Post-Traumatic Stress Disorder (PTSD) relating to my early childhood experiences.

Therapy ... helped me begin to untangle the psychological mess I was left with from childhood and understand the disease of alcoholism and addiction ... [but] it still didn't address my neurochemical problems brought on by PTSD and depression. I still coped with relationship anxiety and psychological triggers that would send me back to my deep seated childhood fears of abandonment and abuse. I tried breathwork, yoga, meditation, and countless other techniques, but none could fix the way I felt about myself at the core ...

My friend turned me on to doing magic mushrooms ... As my first trip began, I wasn't sure what to expect, but as it progressed it developed into an incredibly profound and healing experience. Initially the medicine created a beautiful euphoria of a drug high but it allowed me a safe place to explore the inner workings of my mind like never before. It allowed me to detach myself from my past and evaluate it without triggering the deep emotional upheaval that accompanied my painful memories. As the trip continued new sensations and realizations came about ...

Without fail the medicine took me directly to the root of my pain. It showed me related memories and trauma like sequences of a film. The loneliness I felt got heavier and heavier until I began to cry. My tears brought on an incredible feeling of reconciliation and what followed was a vision of my mother and father. This vision created a warm sensation that took over my body. It was the feeling of pure love and at that moment I could feel the eternal loneliness I had carried for so long disappear. I felt complete and perfectly whole and as the experience drew to a close I felt as if something changed. Something clicked.

In the weeks that followed I could tell that the experience

changed me. The world seemed much more beautiful – colors were brighter and more vivid. I felt recharged and energized and my depression began to vanish ... [E]ach subsequent session with psilocybin relieved more and more of my pain, slowly peeling back the layers of trauma. With each session I found a new relief – my symptoms minimized ...

As I started my fourth trip I immediately felt sick. I held back the need to vomit initially and what followed was five hours of hell and insanity. Confused and disoriented I struggled through one of the toughest nights of my life as I tumbled into a dark psychological abyss. Upon wakening the next morning, I was still in a state of confusion. I didn't understand what went wrong or why I had the traditional "bad trip." As I went on with daily life, normal everyday things seemed new and unfamiliar. It was as if I was re-experiencing life again for the first time. As the months went by I began to realize what had happened. I was no longer being triggered by my past, my PTSD had completely gone away. Arguments or disagreements no longer caused anxiety or flashbacks. The old me had completely died, and along with it had gone my past psychological triggers and depression. I realized that what I perceived to be the worst experience of my life was actually the best, most healing night of my life.

Psilocybin gave me back what was taken so long ago. It gave me back the ability to be vulnerable, and the ability to love and experience life with grace, faith and acceptance. It helped me come back to myself, the real me, deep down, underneath all the fear and hurt. Since my time with psilocybin, I have made some incredible life changes and I am now committed to telling people my story of healing.

The following shorter, more straightforward account, concerns the healing of an Obsessive Compulsive Disorder.

> Ever since I was eight, I have had EXTREME Obsessive Compulsive Disorder. It was horrible, I would have to do EVERYTHING five times all the time. I couldn't sit still for more than five minutes ... eventually, because of my untreated OCD, I was "released" from my job as manager of a diner.
>
> One evening I was reading a report that psilocybin can help cure OCD. So I ordered a mushroom kit, and after about two months, had one ounce dried magic mushrooms. [At my next OCD attack] I consumed two tablespoons of crushed mushrooms [and] after about 10 minutes, the attack completely stopped, like dead in its track. I experienced a mild buzz, but nothing to inhibit my daily activities. The next day, I noticed an amazing thing: I had no OCD attacks. None at all ... [but] the day after that, the attacks came back. Again, I consumed two tablespoons, and about 10 minutes later, they disappeared.
>
> So, with that I made my conclusion ... two tablespoons daily of mushrooms stops my OCD attacks. It has been five months since I started this treatment, and each day I start my morning with two tablespoons of mushrooms.

Finally, here is an account from Darryl, a student who relates how mushrooms not only healed him but literally changed his life, although so deep was the healing that it took him three years to understand all that "Los Ninos" showed him.

> More than two decades ago I had taken magic mushrooms in Australia, in what I now consider a social situation as opposed to a ceremonial one. It would be many years before I would co-lead a ceremony with *teōnanācatl*, the sacred mushroom, and my experiences in ceremony were far different from those social excursions I undertook with my friends all those years ago. Working with plants in a shamanic way has given me a spiritual connection to the mushrooms and their magic,

which back then I did not have. The guidance and healings I have received and witnessed in others have been beautiful. The Mazatec shaman Maria Sabina called these mushrooms *Los Ninos* – the children. This medicine brings back the joy to life, the ability to play, as children do and, as I heard Ross sing in the last ceremonies we held in Scandinavia, "When I was a child I had absolute faith."

We have held ceremonies here for three years so I have been able to see first-hand just how much change takes place when working with this medicine. Participants have told me that their relationships have improved, that they have found answers to difficult problems, made realizations about their abilities and talents and, perhaps most importantly, discovered that there can be joy in their lives. From this it is easy to see that Los Ninos is indeed a medicine and not just a drug as some people label it. From my point of view I can honestly say there has been a change for the better after connecting with this medicine. My creative processes have been opened up in a way I never expected and I am now, after nearly a decade, painting again. My healing work has found the next step I was looking for and my own healing has been extensive.

When we experience trauma it is said by shamans that we fracture and split energetically. The term soul retrieval is one that covers the regaining of lost soul pieces. A healing of the fractures in the energy bodies is what brings back wholeness. The trauma can be emotional, mental or physical in nature. It was after my first ceremony with Los Ninos that I became aware of an emotional, psychological trauma that I had been carrying for eight years. After my parents died and the family home was sold I was not in a good way. About 18 months later I was given soul retrieval from a woman who is top of her game. I have seen her work and been amazed at the information that she is able to access. Yet in my session I thought she was bullshitting because I did not remember any of the things she told me about. "I see you dressed in a suit," she said. "You are caught between places and do not know where to go. Lost." I dismissed it because I just did not recall that event in my life.

Ironically, as I later found out, not remembering is a classic symptom of soul loss, so it was not until six months later that I woke up one morning and suddenly knew exactly what she was talking about. It had been some years ago when I was wearing the suit she described. I had been lost, looking for an address I thought I knew, but I had been wrong. I was running late to meet the lawyer who was holding the probate for my mother and it was the meeting where I had to sign the papers to sell my family home. It would be another six years before I fully understood the impact of that event on me. During those six years I would experience ayahuasca and San Pedro ceremonies for the first time, which gave me deep and profound healings, yet neither of them brought me close to the insight I was to get with Los Ninos.

It was after our first mushroom ceremony and I was walking in the hills nearby, still in pretty good effect that memories began to come back and ideas began to form. It was the first time I had helped to lead a mushroom ceremony and it was what I had been looking for as a next step in my healing work. I began to realize that I now had a commitment to working with plant medicine in ceremony. Mushrooms was one master power plant I would work with, the one for the inner landscape; San Pedro would be the other, for the outer landscape.

It was then that the real insight unfolded. My father had bred and trained racehorses and our family home had 64 stables out back. In my teens I had felt the weight of taking up the family business and began to work with my dad in a more conscious way with the horses. He was an equine genius when it came to breeding and caring for these animals. He said it was a job that had to be in your blood. I understood this because I would see him all my life get up at 3am and work till about 6 or 7pm every day of the week. It was not a typical 9 to 5 job, it was a total commitment of time and energy. This was not a problem for him because he loved his work. I was not an equine genius though; I knew that, so it was with a kind of reluctance that I gave it up.

Many moons later I founded an arts collective and for about 10 years I had the idea that when my father was too old to continue and there would be no more horses I would, with my brother's help, convert the stables into art studios. There was enough space to do a lot of things and it would keep the family home intact and the memory of my father going, since he had built those stables from scratch. So in my heart I had my future planned out.

Which brings me back to that soul retrieval session and a glimpse at where my real trauma was. After dealing with the loss of my mother and father I also had to deal with my brother's greed, as a consequence of which, despite our plans, we ended up selling the family property. The shaman during my soul retrieval had seen the moment before I was to sign the papers for this to happen. I left Australia after that and came to Europe and I was broken. I traveled around looking for something I could not seem to find. Going from country to country from situation to situation was no solution. So here I was seeing this clearly now – the depth of a wound I had carried for eight years. When I had sold the property I had also sold my future. All the plans I had held so dearly in my heart were signed away that day in the lawyer's office.

That mushroom ceremony now helped me access my real future, the one working with plant medicine and healing others through a new practice I began to develop called the Resonant Performer Technique. Suddenly I was no longer lost. I knew what I wanted to do with my life. I felt happy.

Other insights I have got with this medicine have been incredible in many ways. One took three years to unfold. In that first Scandinavian ceremony I had the vision of being amongst light blue strands. Within those strands were pockets of space and in those spaces I was seeing things that I knew were important to my spirituality. It was a little while afterwards that I realized I had been inside the mycelium, the root system of the mushrooms. Three years later, on the last of our valedas in 2017 one of the participants, Peter, came to me after the ceremony and said, "I have left a gift for Ross somewhere." I asked him where and what it was but as he was still in strong effect all he could tell me was that it was "Somewhere" and that it was "A gift for Ross that he can get the next time he is in ceremony." I guess I might have shaken my head wondering what he was on about but I knew he was earnest and not delirious.

It was about two months later that I was skyping with a friend in Barcelona. "Oh man," he said, "We had a mushroom ceremony here on the weekend and it was crazy. The mushrooms told me I could leave a message for my kids." He then went on to describe that he had left information for his children in pockets of mycelium and if they ever took mushrooms they would be able to access it. Bingo I thought, this sounds familiar. "Was it in pockets between the blue strands?" I asked him. "Yes, in the mycelium and the mushrooms said it would be there for when they come to look for it."

Then I totally understood what I had seen in my own ceremony and I knew what Peter had been saying too. Both had left something for someone in pockets of space in the mycelium just as I had seen information there for me amongst the blue strands. *We can access psychic data from the storehouse that is the mycelium system, or better still the mycelium is a kind of*

> *psycho-spiritual library. Los Ninos are guardians of a kind of living information which we can gain access to through intention.* So just imagine the information that may have been left by people in ancient times working with the medicine for those of us who come to the mushrooms now. Los Ninos have many secrets to tell for people who are serious in their quest and not just taking mushrooms for a good time.

"Language makes the dying return to life," said Maria Sabina. "The sick recover their health when they hear the words taught by the saint children. There is no mortal who can teach this language."

Physical Cures

Unlike the preceding accounts which concern emotional or mental problems, those that follow suggest the ability of magic mushrooms to heal physical ailments too, some of which medical science struggles to provide help for at all.

Cluster Headache 1

"I am a long time chronic sufferer of cluster headaches. I had recently stumbled upon a website that said LSD or magic mushrooms helped with cluster headaches. I immediately called a friend to get some mushrooms. Before I go further I must state I have tried a lot of RX [standard pharmaceutical] drugs to try to combat the enormous amount of pain I go through daily. I [added] one mushroom to a cup of [hot] water drinking slowly over a half hour. It has been a month since I have had a headache, very mild ones maybe twice in the month. I can't describe the absolute bliss I have towards life now. No pills with all the risk! I am glad I stumbled upon that info [about mushrooms]. The world must know the medicinal effects of mushrooms!!"

Cluster Headache 2

"[My] attacks would start very fast and without warning about three times a day, almost always occurring in the early hours of the morning and would last for a couple of hours. My mom took me to several doctors, including a neurologist. I was diagnosed with cluster headaches and prescribed many different types of medication that did not work. The only medicine that even dulled my symptoms were opiates, which would not completely stamp out the problem.

"I did some research and, to my surprise, found that psilocybin was a possible effective cluster headache treatment. I mentioned this to my mom and got what I expected: a firm disapproval. Being an experienced user of psychedelics, I decided to make a trip to the fields the next time it rained and harvested many fresh Cubensis mushrooms. My friend and I ate around eight fresh mushrooms (approximately 3 grams dried) and had a great trip. The next night I had a full eight hours of sleep with no cluster headache attack and haven't had one since. I hope this information helps with [creating awareness of] psilocybin for the treatment and elimination of cluster headaches."

Migraine

"I have suffered from chronic, debilitating migraines since the onset of puberty and I am now 48 years old. I have tried traditional medicine, acupuncture, homeopathy, chiropractic and herbal remedies, without success. At times, these migraines last for 3–5 days, and can recur several times a month.

"I have experimented with both psilocybin and LSD in the past, and when doing research, I discovered that both substances were being considered for medical research into cluster headaches and migraines. After reading this information, I decided to use psilocybin in an attempt to prevent/reduce the frequency and intensity of my migraines …

"I consciously create a pleasant, relaxed environment with

low lighting and good music, in the comfort of my own home. Most of the time, I have used Mexican Cubensis alone, but have used them with a friend on occasion. During this time I have used them approximately every 7–10 days. I have not used them during a migraine, but rather when I was not in pain. I choose Cubensis because they are relatively freely available and inexpensive. I used a dosage of 7 grams each time, because that was the dosage I had previously used recreationally. In addition, I know that I have a high tolerance for prescription medication and recreation drugs alike. I generally make a tea with them, using hot water and honey to extract the active ingredient …

"All of my experiences with Cubensis have been extremely pleasant. On several occasions I have found myself basking in pure light. I have felt a sense of connectedness with the universe, felt a sense of 'falling into eternity' and journeyed into realms of colorful symbols, and seen vivid geometrical structures in the sky and in my room. I have also perceived a sense of multidimensional reality. Music has become a multi-sensory experience of color, symbols, vivid images, texture and occasionally even smells.

"The results of this experiment have transcended the original goal in many ways. First of all, I did experience a dramatic decrease in frequency and duration of migraines. During the three-month period I only experienced two migraines as opposed to the usual 10–12. Instead of lasting 3–5 days, the two migraines I did get, only lasted 24–36 hours. Aside from this, I noticed the following emotional/psychological/spiritual effects: greater empathy for people (I work as a counselor), more patience, increased sense of inner peace, creative problem solving strategies come to mind more readily, spiritually I frequently feel a sense of oneness with the universe … Since doing my own 'clinical trial,' I have not needed to request refills for prescriptions related to migraines such as painkillers (Tylenol 3 and Toradol), medication to stop an attack (Ergotamine a.k.a. Cafergot) or Beta Blockers."

Migraine 2

"From late childhood to when I was 16, I suffered from migraines … I was 16 when I first-time tripped on mushrooms and what struck me was that I was used to the pain cycle of having a migraine every fortnight [but this had not happened for] several months after my initial trip. I concluded that I could only attribute it to my trips on psilocybin. I then embarked on a journey of six years of psychonautic exploration [during which] I had NO migraines.

"[I then did less psychedelics] a very few number of times until winter 2003–2004, and all of 2004 I have had violent [migraine] attacks [again]. I then dosed myself with fresh handpicked [mushrooms] and have had no migraines since. I am now back on track [and] more ready than ever to preach the gospel of entheogens."

Fibromyalgia

"Having suffered from fibromyalgia in its many guises since childhood … I was still blown away in my 30s by the searing pain of the combination of fibromyalgia and early menopause. My living, mothering, self-esteem, and material world slipped away as I turned to alcohol nightly to dull my over-amped central nervous system just so I could sleep, and thus function.

"Fibromyalgia is a complex syndrome of the central nervous system, which amplifies all sensory input, especially pain. Research is just beginning to unravel the complex abnormal endocrine system and brain chemistry of the fibromite. The complex of neurotransmitters that regulate sleep and mood, including serotonin and melatonin tend to be low, creating long-term sleep deprivation of the deeper cellular-repairing stages of sleep. The lack of restorative sleep leaves the patient achy, stiff and painful, with the pain and accompanying symptoms moving throughout the body and changing moment to moment. Irritable bowel syndrome, another fun pain condition, is more often than not present. Fibro folks feel pain from normal stimuli, including lights, sounds, smells, and chemicals. They're the proverbial Princess and the Pea people – the body's electrical system tends to always be set on high, in constant fight or flight. The other primary common feature of the disease is what's called 'brain fog,', or an accompanying lack of cognitive skills, including memory loss during pain flares or episodes, which can last from hours to weeks to months, essentially rendering one non-functional and unable to attend to even the simplest tasks of living. What all the lack of sleep and pain, plus many other seemingly unrelated symptoms (including low immune function) means is that we usually feel like we're about to jump out of our skin at the drop of a pin. Not a fun way to live, and a huge frustration to loved ones who can't 'see' the disability. We fibro folks tend to not go out in public much during flares.

"Two years ago, I was gifted with a box of mushroom chocolates for my birthday. Dried Psilocybin cubensis was ground up then mixed into the most decadent organic dark melted chocolate, then poured into tiny ice cube trays to create uniform candies to delight the soul. At my 100 lbs, a whole chocolate would've sent me into the nether worlds, so I saved them for a special occasion. Meantime, my physical functioning continued to deteriorate ...

"One night, one of my favorite, not-to-be-missed bands was in town and I was determined to go dance, even if I had to pay in after-pain for days ... Then I remembered the chocolates. I decided to take a very small 'homeopathic' nibble for some stable body energy while dancing, though I didn't wish to 'trip' or be otherwise psychedelically altered. One little bite to melt in my mouth and forget about. By the time I'd had just one beer, I was relaxed and engaged enough with the music to hit the dance floor. Danced all night, drank water to hydrate, drove home, went straight to sleep like a baby. Next day, I got up and went about my business as if I hadn't danced like a fool for hours and hours the night before ... and I WASN'T IN PAIN. The next few times I got a wild hair to dance, I followed essentially the same protocol. Never any painful after-burn for the days following.

"I began to notice this pattern and wonder if in fact the small doses of psilocybin are a natural painkiller … Wow. Most fibromites I know are pharmaceutically medicated with a standard protocol, including: sleeping pills, painkillers and antidepressants. Being chemically sensitive, I simply cannot take these meds … Now I feel like I have a new tool."

Back Pain

"My fiancée and I managed to get a hold of a free sample (-2g) of some mushrooms my friend had just harvested from his own growing experiment … The trip was very mellow due to the fairly low dose. Very warm feelings overcame us, we laughed a ton, and just generally felt very happy [read: ecstatic] … However, the most interesting thing I've noticed regarding this particular voyage, was that as I was returning to baseline, my lower back pain had completely subsided. Back in July, I was injured at work which resulted in several strained muscles and a lower back sprain, with frequent painful back spasms. The pain was constant for nearly a month and a half …

"As we were returning to normal, I noticed that the muscles in my back had completely relaxed to a point where they felt almost squishy [and] upon waking the next morning I realized that I was not completely stiff and immobile, but was actually somewhat limber … as the day went on, it felt increasingly better, to the point where I didn't need to take anything for the pain (ibuprofen 800mg).

"I am writing this on Sunday morning (a week later) and the pain has been minimal all week, with hardly any need of the [painkiller] Motrin. Not to mention that back spasms have been significantly reduced. In hindsight, the next day, I also realized that I was not limping the whole night after the mushrooms had kicked in … Amazing stuff."

Medical Research

The preceding accounts are powerful because they are personal. They give us an insight into the nature and intensity of the mushroom experience because they are *real*. Someone actually *felt this* and was affected by it. Science, however, is not interested in feelings or personal stories but in objectivity and number-crunching. It believes, strangely, that statistics and calculus can provide us with a better account of human experience than human experience can. And yet, even science has found itself impressed by studies which show the ability of psilocybin to help people heal from conditions including depression, anxiety, addiction and post-traumatic stress disorder (PTSD).

Depression

On December 1, 2016 *The Guardian* newspaper carried the story, *Magic mushroom chemical psilocybin could be key to treating depression.*[36] "A single dose of psilocybin, the active ingredient of magic mushrooms," it said, "can lift the anxiety and depression experienced by people with advanced cancer for six months or even longer, two new studies show. Researchers involved in the two trials in the United States say the results are remarkable. The volunteers had 'profoundly meaningful and spiritual experiences' which made most of them rethink life and death, ended their despair and brought about lasting improvement in the quality of their lives."

Fifty percent of newly diagnosed cancer patients suffer depression or anxiety and many contemplate suicide, feeling that their lives are meaningless. Antidepressants have little effect. The new studies, however, involving 29 patients and 51 patients respectively, found that a single dose of psilocybin produced an immediate reduction in depression and anxiety and the effect could last up to eight months. Eighty percent of patients attributed their improved well-being and life satisfaction to this single dose of the drug.

One explanation for this is that psilocybin activates a serotonin receptor in the brain to produce what one of the researchers called "spiritual states, mystical states ... defined by a sense of oneness – people feel that their separation between the personal ego and the outside world is sort of dissolved and they feel that they are part of some continuous energy or consciousness in the universe. Patients can feel sort of transported to a different dimension of reality, sort of like a waking dream." Some subjects describe seeing images from their childhood and/or of a confrontation with their cancer during these dream states. They were then able to challenge, change and embrace these life events and pass through them to a more uplifting resolution.

Anxiety

An article from December 2016 – *The fascinating, strange medical potential of psychedelic drugs explained in 50+ studies* – by German Lopez and Javier Zarracina[37] relates another success with a cancer patient, this time in curing the anxiety associated with the disease.

> After years of struggling with treatments for his worsening cancer, Roy was miserable – anxious, depressed, hopeless. Traditional cancer treatments had left him debilitated and it was unclear whether they would save his life. But then Roy secured a spot in a clinical trial to test an exotic drug. The drug was not meant to cure his cancer; it was meant to cure his terror. And it worked. A few hours after taking a little pill, Roy declared to researchers "Cancer is not important, the important stuff is love." His concerns about his imminent death had suddenly vanished – and the effects lasted for at least months.
>
> It was not a traditional antidepressant, like Zoloft, or anti-anxiety medication, like Xanax, that led Roy to re-evaluate his life. It was a drug that has been illegal for decades but

is now at the center of a renaissance in research: psilocybin, from hallucinogenic magic mushrooms.

After hearing of the success of Roy in overcoming his anxiety, the authors of this article read more than 50 studies analyzing the safety and efficacy of psychedelics in providing treatment and benefits to a variety of sufferers, and talked to researchers involved in this work. A few of their conclusions are that:

- The mystical dimension of psychedelics is what makes them therapeutic.

  "Here is a small sampling of how some participants in several studies since the 2000s described [their] experiences: 'Feelings of gratefulness, a great (powerful) remembrance of humility ... of my being in and within the infinite.' 'I believe I channeled the power of the Goddess and that I hold that power in me. I believe she exists everywhere and I look for her to add spark, life, and joy to everyday ordinary situations.' 'The experience expanded my conscious awareness permanently. It allows me to let go of negative ideas faster. I accept "what is" easier.' 'My conversation with God (golden streams of light) assuring me that everything on this plane is perfect; but I do not have the physical body/mind to fully understand.' It may be easy to dismiss these experiences. What do gods and golden streams of light have to do with medicine? But the findings from many studies, which can involve months or years of follow-up, are promising ... One very small study of 15 smokers found [for example, that] 12 (80 percent) managed to abstain from smoking for six months after a psilocybin treatment ... [It also] helped people diagnosed with alcohol dependence [to] cut back on their drinking days. Another study found that psilocybin may have helped treat depression for patients who had proven resistant to other treatments.

"So how exactly are psychedelics achieving this? Researchers readily admit that they don't have all the answers ... But drawing on the current studies and the research from the '50s and '60s, they have a theory: When people are faced with debilitating mental conditions, psychedelics ... can trigger a powerful mystical experience. The experience can then provide a psychological context that makes positive behavioral change easier. 'They have profound, meaningful experiences that can sometimes help them make new insights into their own behaviors and also to reconnect with their values and priorities in terms of what's important to them in the grander scheme of things,' Albert Garcia-Romeu, [a] Johns Hopkins researcher, said. 'When they have those kinds of experiences, it seems to be helpful for people to be able to make behavior changes down the line, like quitting smoking.'"

In the studies, it only took one or two doses of psilocybin to produce months of benefits, unlike psychiatric medications that often require daily doses for months or years. The amount of benefit also increased according to the depth of the mystical connection. Dr Johnson of Johns Hopkins said, "We found that the degree of mystical experience ... is predictive of long-term beneficial effects – of reductions in anxiety and depression [and] reductions in cigarette smoking. One way of understanding the effect is by looking at it as the opposite of a traumatic experience."

- The mystical experience is one of greater connectivity, resulting in healing.

"British researchers have used imaging techniques to gauge how the brain looks on psychedelics versus a placebo [and] they found big differences," say the authors. The brain on psychedelics shows much more connectivity between its different sections, which is precisely why psychedelics are able to help people. "In many psychiatric disorders, the brain may be viewed as having become entrenched in pathology, such that core behaviors become automated and rigid," the researchers wrote. "Psychedelics may work to break down such disorders by dismantling the patterns of activity on which they rest."

- Psychedelics treat the person's *context*, not just his illness.

  "My personal opinion is that the reason these [anxiety and depression-producing] conditions are so hard to treat from a standard medical perspective is that there's something more to them than just the illness," says Dr Garcia-Romeu, pointing to addiction as an example. "Oftentimes we have to do actual therapy. We can't just give them a pill to make their problems go away. We have to really delve into things like childhood trauma and current life situations and relationships and whether those relationships are healthy or toxic and how people feel about themselves." This can all take time, and it also confounds the standard scientific model which would prefer to ignore any spiritual, mental or emotional dimensions to life and focus solely on the material, treating physical-only disorders with physical-only methods, i.e. pills not counseling. Thankfully, it appears that the counseling can be left to psilocybin so that doctors don't have to trouble themselves with it for, as Garcia-Romeu points out, "Psychedelics are a very rapid way to induce very meaningful change in people."

- There are few risks to psychedelic drugs.

In fact, the authors state the opposite, that, "There are some big risks to psychedelic drugs," but I'm not sure where they got this idea since they go on to say that, "A review of the research in 1999 found [that psychedelics] don't appear to cause personality changes or other chronic psychological issues … One study on psilocybin and a review of the psychedelic literature found no major physical effects besides dizziness, headaches, and exhaustion for a few days after use." Basically, if you are sensible and responsible and act maturely and respectfully towards psilocybin mushrooms (choosing to follow the guidance in this book, for example) the chances of you encountering immediate or lasting problems are slim to none.

- The use of psychedelics may benefit all of us, not just the gravely ill.

  The authors point out that, "Currently, psychedelic research is focused on the truly ill. But there's no obvious reason to believe the benefits are solely limited to that group. After all, almost everyone deals with some anxiety related to death. Psychedelics could help relieve that anxiety. As Mark Kleiman, a drug policy expert at the New York University's Marron Institute, previously told me, 'The obvious application [of psychedelics] is people who are currently dying with a terminal diagnosis. But being born is a terminal diagnosis. And people's lives might be better if they live out of the valley of the shadow of death.'"

  Some studies have validated this. One, in 2011, by Johns Hopkins found that people who reported psilocybin-induced mystical experiences showed more openness in personality tests which might in turn lead to better life experiences and quality of life. As if to confirm this, other Johns Hopkins studies in 2008 and 2011 noted that psilocybin users reported higher life satisfaction and positive moods, particularly among those who described the most powerful mystical experiences, leading researchers to suggest that "many people could potentially benefit from psychedelic-assisted therapy, even if they don't have a severe, diagnosed disorder or condition."

"Most of psychology and medicine are, believe it or not, focused on the negative. The only time you go see a psychologist is if you have a mental illness, or the only time you go see a doctor is because you're sick," Dr Garcia-Romeu said. "But that's 50 percent of the spectrum. The other 50 percent of the spectrum [is] people who are well or are even optimal, functioning at a higher than average level. And I think those people who are just fine … can certainly benefit from these types of experiences [too]."

- Psychedelic research exposes a big flaw in drug policy and funding.

"The early research in this field [of psilocybin-assisted healing] is promising enough that many researchers and experts are taking it very seriously and aggressively pursuing additional studies. But much of the work has been snared by regulatory barriers," the authors comment. "The classic psychedelics are Schedule 1 substances, meaning the federal government deems them to have no medical use and high potential for abuse. With that schedule comes unique restrictions [which] can all add months or years – [and] higher financial costs – to a study. Another major hurdle is funding … After widespread psychedelic abuse in the 1960s [sic], a huge cultural and political backlash to these drugs killed most federal funding. Now federally funded studies on psychedelics focus on these substances' dangers, not their potential benefits. After all, the feds don't even acknowledge that these drugs have any medical value to begin with …

"This leaves it to private organizations to fund much of the psychedelics research with the help of private donations … The result [so far] is we have a lot of anecdotes, like Roy's, and some smaller studies that show psychedelic drugs' promise for treating some crippling medical conditions. The holes in our knowledge, however, could be easily filled. There's more than enough promise here to merit further research and further funding for that research."

Post-Traumatic Stress Disorder

An article by Jason Louv reports that psilocybin can cure PTSD, erase conditioned fear responses and even grow new brain cells.[38]

"According to a study conducted at the University of South Florida, low doses of psilocybin mushrooms erase the conditioned fear response in mice – which, the researchers suggest, may lead to the potential treatment of PTSD ... The unexpected finding was made by a USF team studying the effects of the compound psilocybin on the birth of new neurons in the brain and on learning and short-term memory formation. Their study appeared online June 2 in the journal *Experimental Brain Research* ...

"Psilocybin belongs to a class of compounds that stimulate select serotonin receptors in the brain. 'It occurs naturally in certain mushrooms that have been used for thousands of years by non-Western cultures in their religious ceremonies,' said Juan Sanchez-Ramos, professor of neurology at the USF Health Morsani College of Medicine. 'While past studies indicate psilocybin may alter perception and thinking and elevate mood ... Researchers [also] want to find out if at lower doses these drugs could be safe and effective additions to psychotherapy for treatment-resistant psychiatric disorders or adjunct treatments for certain neurological conditions.'"

Conclusion

These are just a few of the possible treatment applications for psilocybin and one of the reasons why news stories containing new and positive research results with this plant-derived chemical seem to appear almost daily. If governments would now begin to sponsor properly objective studies into psilocybin instead of ones intent on discovering new "dangers" from it in order to justify policy, these positive results would inevitably come thicker and faster, and the future for sufferers from a range of sicknesses and disorders – depression, anxiety, PTSD and addictions among them – would quickly start to look brighter.

5

Conclusions and Cautions: Working Responsibly with Mushrooms

Magic mushrooms are the safest "recreational" drug and those who take them are the most sensible and well prepared, according to the 2017 Global Drug Survey [GDS]. Out of almost 10,000 people who took them, only 0.2% needed emergency medical treatment. But magic mushrooms, or psilocybin mushrooms, contain a compound that has been a class A drug under the UK Misuse of Drugs Act since 1971 – like heroin and crack cocaine.
Luisa Dillner[39]

The fact that only 0.2% of mushroom users required medical help makes mushrooms, on this rating at least, safer than synthetic cannabis (3.2% of users needing medical help) and alcohol (1.3% of users needing help).[40] In fact mushrooms are the safest "drug" of all on the GDS scale, and yet psilocybin remains class A. This contradiction is even more bizarre when you consider the number of fatalities each year from perfectly legal state-approved drugs. For example:

- Alcohol: "Excessive alcohol use is a leading cause of preventable death [accounting] for approximately 88,000 deaths per year [and] 1 in 10 deaths among working-age adults aged 20–64 years. Excessive alcohol use shortened the lives of those who died by about 30 years" – CDC.[41]
- Cigarettes: "Cigarette smoking causes about one of every five deaths in the United States each year [i.e. 20% of deaths]. Cigarette smoking is estimated to cause … more than 480,000 deaths annually" – Centers for Disease Control and Prevention (CDC).[42]

- Prescription medications: "The United States is in the midst of a prescription painkiller overdose epidemic. Since 1999, the amount of prescription painkillers prescribed and sold in the US has nearly quadrupled, yet there has not been an overall change in the amount of pain that Americans report. Overprescribing leads to more abuse and more overdose deaths. Every day, 44 people in the US die from overdose of prescription painkillers, and many more become addicted" – CDC.[43]

The *Guardian* article continues: "Dr Robin Carhart-Harris, head of psychedelic research at Imperial College, London, explains that … shrooms can make you euphoric, at one with the world and searingly insightful... Carhart-Harris says magic mushrooms are not really recreational drugs: 'It's more a drug of self-exploration,' he says. The environment, though, is essential to having a positive experience – people need space, a 'sober sitter' to take care of them – and they may need reassurance that they are not going mad. Carhart-Harris prefers the term 'challenging experience' over 'bad trip': mushrooms can cause anxiety, panic and depersonalisation[44] but studies show people still value the experience as meaningful.

"Studies do not show increased mental health problems from habitual use – unlike the effects of cocaine or cannabis. A *BMJ* [British Medical Journal] article by psychiatrist James J. H. Rucker argues that psychedelic drugs may actually help depression and that there is no association with psychosis. A paper in science journal *PLoS One* found no evidence of flashbacks (such as hallucinations or panic attacks) from sole mushroom use. Mushrooms aren't habit forming and are far less toxic to our internal organs than heroin or cocaine. However, ***you should not take them*** as they are against the law and this article is not promoting their use in any way … Carhart-Harris researches into the benefits of psychedelic drugs on depression, and says that most experiences on mushrooms are positive ... [and yet] ***young people in particular should stay away.*** 'They are not for teenagers,' he warns. 'They make you psychologically vulnerable and you need the capacity to make sense of the experience.'"

The italics in bold are mine, to illustrate how preposterous the current legal situation still is regarding mushrooms and the aura of moral panic which still surrounds their use. According to the experts the *Guardian* quotes there is *no* danger from magic mushrooms; in fact, medical research shows that they *help* with certain debilitating conditions. Carhart-Harris tells us they provide "benefits" and that "most experiences ... are positive." Yet the author of this article, Luisa Dillner, still warns us away from using them. Why? Because "they are against the law." "If the law supposes that," to quote Dickens, then "the law is an ass – an idiot. If that's the eye of the law ... the worst I wish the law is that his eye may be opened by experience." I wish the same for Dillner, that her eyes are opened by experience too so that she doesn't kowtow to ridiculous laws in future, just because they are laws. Meanwhile other "drugs," like booze, tobacco and prescription meds, cause serious health problems, bring few or no benefits and remain totally legal.

I am also puzzled by Carhart-Harris' claim that teenagers should never take mushrooms. Based on what evidence, especially when he himself reports "mostly positive" experiences for users? His rather patronising statement that you need the "[mental] capacity" to make sense of the mushroom experience is no justification for his claim but rather assumes that young people are universally stupid and lacking in judgment and mental alacrity. In the real world, however, in Mexico I have seen children as young as seven in mushroom ceremonies; in the Andes of Peru, toddlers join San Pedro ceremonies (though they don't always drink or drink only a drop of the medicine) and in Amazon tribes it is customary for the first drink of ayahuasca to be taken at the age of 13 as an initiation into manhood. I see no reason why teenagers should be singled out as incapable and refused entry to a properly managed and supervised ceremony. In fact, with all the demands and confusions facing teenagers in our modern plastic world, a mushroom ceremony would probably do them good, opening them up to the sacred, the magic of the Earth and the purpose of their lives beyond their never-ending conditioned consumption of iPhones and selfies.

There are certain pre-existing physical conditions where caution with magic mushrooms is recommended but overall and in general the risks from working with this plant are minimal. Physically, psilocybin at high doses tends to increase heart rate and lower blood pressure so people with heart or blood pressure conditions need to take care. As regards mental health concerns, "There is no evidence that mushrooms can make a healthy subject psychotic," says Andy Letcher. "Latent psychosis could be triggered [however], for even alcohol can bring latent mental illness to the fore. PET scans of the brain have shown that most psilocybin activity occurs in the areas of the brain known as the prefrontal cortex, the anterior cingulate and the tempromedial cortex ... these same areas are implicated in certain types of schizophrenia [so] it stands to reason that anyone with a personal or family history of mental illness or who is depressed or feeling psychologically unstable in any way should assiduously avoid mushrooms or any other psychoactive drugs for that matter." Think back to what Jenn achieved for her student by not checking her medical history and allowing drug use on her property prior to a badly-run ceremony. If the user is healthy in mind and body, however, experts agree that there is nothing in mushrooms *per se*, or the mushroom experience which is likely to change that.

Ceremonial Precautions

Despite the documented lack of ill-effects from taking mushrooms, there is still a big difference between conscious exploration and blind, dumb risk-taking; between taking sensible precautions and rushing headfirst into the unknown, so I want to suggest a few safeguards here, especially if this is your first time.

Firstly, know what you're getting into. Mushrooms are not a "recreational drug." They are a sacred medicine, capable of facilitating deep healing and a profound shift in consciousness if you approach them with clear intention and treat them with respect. If you choose not to ... well, we get the mushroom trip we deserve.

The best way to work with mushrooms is in ceremony with a shaman who knows the medicine and understands what you're going through so he can help you if you need some support. If that is really not possible, at least have a sitter with you who has some experience with psilocybin and can help you practically and emotionally (if needed) during your journey.

In chapter 2, I set out my approach to ceremony, which you can adapt if you want and add your own respectful innovations to it if you are in charge of the event. These are the basics:

- Follow a proper shamanic diet prior to the event and have your participants do the same. At the very least, fast on the day of the ceremony. There are instructions for dieting in my other plant medicine books and at my website, www.thefourgates.org[45]
- Create a safe, sacred space by making prayers to the saints, to the spirit of the mushrooms and to the other helpful spirits you wish to watch over you, then seal the space you have made, using a rattle, a temple bell, by chanting or by using incense to smudge the air, etc., as you walk the entire room with the intention of "owning" it and excluding any unwanted spiritual guests.
- Light a candle before a statue of the Virgin which you should position to watch over participants.
- Then hand each person a share of mushrooms (I always of-

fer cacao beans and a glass of tequila as well). You should eat and drink in silence while focusing on your intention for healing, and encourage everyone present not to speak or move during the night.

- My ceremonies normally start at around 8pm and continue until the next day. I sit with a *mesa* (a small cloth altar) and make prayers, hymns and songs in order to maintain a sacred space and keep the focus on the holy and on healing. I conduct a healing for each person present and make prayers before the altar for those who are absent but still in need of help.
- I close the ceremony by offering a prayer of thanks to the spirits who have watched over us, and then release them from our ceremony.

If your event is less formal or you are not running a ceremony but just taking mushrooms for your own self-exploration, it is still good practice to pay attention to set and setting, and to make your prayers before you begin and after you close your circle. This shows respect to the spirits whose help you are seeking and helps ensure that you stay focused on your purpose.

The account below, by another of my students, is a good "How To" guide for working with mushrooms as a solo traveler and illustrates the healing possible from following proper precautions.

> My experience of psilocybin is that of teacher, healer and cosmic traveler. A "Babelfish" of the Upper world, this spirit plant helps you find guides and mentors, fixes your body and opens your inner Star Gate to other dimensions. The next day you feel like you've had an amazing tonic, for indeed you have.
>
> Sixteen years ago, desperate to contact an unknown something in myself, I felt the call, researching how to

identify mushrooms, where they grow and what dosages are required. With book in hand I embarked upon a sacred journey of wonderment, learning and healing, quickly discovering "they are where you find them." In the first instance the local botanical gardens where the ravens were also eating them. No wonder they are spirit birds.

You can brew fresh mushrooms in a herbal tea or extend the season by keeping dried capsules in the freezer. Regardless, I always fast half a day beforehand to enhance efficacy. Without an experienced human mentor, I discovered for myself "shrooms" don't like electric lighting, in fact they possess their own inner light. Secondly, preparing oneself mentally and spiritually aided by fasting gives better outcomes. Unprepared for the intense physical rush, that first journey was both elating and unnerving upon realising I had encountered an Entity and there's no getting off the bus. On the third journey, I cottoned on, relaxed, breathed deeply and simply let the mushrooms in, following them as they tinkered in my body fixing things, chuckling at seeing this collective fluorescent entity with tiny antennae at work. The next day feeling fantastic for having taken this tonic, it dawned on me I could work with them to release and heal buried trauma in my body. During the early physical onset, I concentrate on following psilocybes around my body and work with them before embarking on the main quest.

I love the beautiful rainbow mosaics but it's a trap to be caught in visuals for a deeper visionary journey beckons. Because psilocybin likes to travel and will go anywhere I found it important to take responsibility for the purpose of the journey. I remember once having a tiff with my partner earlier in the day and because the mushrooms were collected we journeyed anyway. Big mistake, as I found myself with darker energies combating lizards and cockroach forms. Filled with contrition, I focused on a figure that had been calling me in my dreams. She showed me the way out of that space. This figure turned out to be a significant teacher and otherworld mentor. I learned two lessons that night, firstly prepare and be in a right space which includes some ceremony and secondly work with your otherworld mentors. Psilocybin specializes in aiding a strong connection with them for longer. With this spirit plant there's time for your mentors to teach and take you into other dimensions for soul work.

Another thing I learned through journeying with spirit plants is our soul bridges both spirit and flesh. We can heal the future by redeeming the past. When working in the lower and upper worlds we're outside of time, returning to earth having affected change in our ordinary reality.

I met Ross attending a spirit plant workshop in Spain where I benefited from his extensive teaching and broad experience with spirit plants. The teaching joined many dots for me. In particular resonating with Ross' explanation of spirit plants activating and healing our DNA. Having personally experienced that, I will cite a couple of examples in ancestor work.

Ancestors have gifts and attributes with which to bless us, though many need resolution first. We carry their DNA in us and by releasing their pain it heals the scarlet thread in us and our descendants. I was taken to an event in the past where Knights Templar ancestors were fighting courageously. My guide took me into the situation with the power to redeem it because I'm mortal, bridging spirit and flesh, so I could act effectively in that dimension. Shown what to do, a curse was broken and positive changes have occurred in my life and those of my family since. Another time I was guided to do soul retrieval for my dead grandfather which had a profound effect on my mother and one of my daughters who is very like her.

As one who needed to heal the severe conditioning of my

upbringing and restore a repressed medial nature, psilocybin has been a faithful teacher opening the doors of perception and forging new neural pathways, restoring ancestral gifts and attributes in the process. This spirit plant is a pathfinder, healer and teacher. It has empowered me to find my true Self, that unknown something I needed to connect with so long ago.

After each journey, energies released and/or found make a profound difference physically, spiritually and emotionally, resulting in personal transformation. The sense of connectedness has become a deeper reality as my ground of being has expanded on this journey of coming home to myself, discovering in the truest, deepest sense that I am loved and here by Grace. The wonderful thing about working with spirit plants is that each person experiences what is best for them.

As Ross is fond of saying "we know nothing" and that is true. The protection of otherworld mentors who know far more than we do are the true magicians with loving hearts and immense compassion for the human condition. Working with them has given me a heart for the broken-hearted and a desire to see others undertake their journey to wholeness. For me it's a lifelong process of pilgrimage and initiation. Having crawled out of a head space the size of a matchbox, I could never go back. Availing oneself of good teaching greatly aids the process of transformation, sparing the traveler some of the scrapes and bruises this ignorant pilgrim endured at times. The journey is worth the effort though, for when you find your inner well, joy flows perennially in the verdant landscape of your soul.

The Legalities of Mushrooms

The legal status of psilocybin mushrooms varies worldwide. Psilocybin and psilocin are listed as Schedule 1 drugs under the

United Nations 1971 Convention on Psychotropic Substances, defining them as having a high potential for abuse and no medical use. This definition is total nonsense, of course since, as we have seen, mushrooms have a significantly *lower* potential for abuse than many legal drugs including alcohol and tobacco, as well as all other Schedule 1 substances. They also have numerous significant and clinically recognized medicinal applications and religious uses in dozens of cultures worldwide throughout thousands of years of history. Even so, many countries have some level of regulation or prohibition, although in practice there is a lot of ambiguity about the exact legal status of mushrooms and often selective enforcement at a state or national level.

The legal status of psilocybe spores is even more ambiguous, as they do not even contain psilocybin or psilocin so they should not be illegal to sell or possess. Some jurisdictions will still prosecute, however, under broader laws prohibiting items that can be used in drug manufacture and a few jurisdictions (such as the US states of Georgia and Idaho) have also specifically prohibited the sale and possession of mushroom spores. Cultivation of psilocybin mushrooms is considered drug manufacture in most jurisdictions, although some more rational states have concluded that *growing mushrooms* is not the same as *manufacturing a controlled substance.*

Wikipedia, often dodgy as a reliable information source, in this case at least has a useful list of countries and their policies regarding mushroom possession, sale, transportation and cultivation at https://en.wikipedia.org/wiki/Legal_status_of_psilocybin_mushrooms

It could (and should) be argued that no government has a natural authority of any kind, through the enactment of laws like these, to try to control your right to explore your own consciousness and engage your own mind. *Whose mind is it anyway?* And then, *how can a plant even be "illegal"?* The idea that it could be is so preposterous that only a governance of fools could arrive at it. *And of what possible harm to others is a healing ceremony using a plant that has been regarded as sacred for millennia, which is attended by informed and consenting, supposedly-free adults with a right to choose for themselves?* The state's obviously money-motivated prejudices against plants like these is hypocritical and despicable when, at the same time, it openly supports drugs like alcohol, tobacco and prescription meds, which collectively harm or kill millions of people each year but make the government a fortune in taxes.

We do not live in enlightened (or even honest and rational) times, that is for sure, but while our legislators would certainly benefit from a healthy dose of mushrooms themselves before throwing their jack-booted legal weight around and making laws about things which they, by definition as law-abiding citizens, know nothing about, that day is surely a long way off.

In the meantime we are free, with quiet dignity, to practice our own form of civil disobedience and claim sovereignty over our minds, hearts, bodies and souls. We are hurting no one by doing so and, in fact, by expanding our awareness through the magical gifts of the mushrooms, we become pioneers adding to the wisdom of this planet. In our spiritual generosity we help even the ignorant by doing so, though they would rather punish than thank us for the help that we give them.

Endnotes

1. Read the full article online here: http://goo.gl/4JrT4w
2. Technically, mushrooms are fungi rather than "plants" and are usually placed in a Kingdom of their own, apart from plants and animals. The word "plant" is used in this book, however, since shamans do not concern themselves with categories and distinctions like these but are more interested in "plant intelligences".
3. Teonanácatl. From *teó* (god, sacred) and *nanácatl* (mushroom) in the Náhuatl language of Mexico.
4. See Ross Heaven, *Plant Spirit Wisdom* (O Books) for more on this story.
5. So giving rise to the name by which sacred and ceremonial mushrooms are best known nowadays: "magic mushrooms".
6. Actually, this is hardly, if ever, true. Mushrooms taste "earthy" (especially if freshly picked), as you would expect; maybe a little "cardboardy," certainly not "bad", and their taste (if any) is fleeting. It does not "repeat." Their smell, if fresh, might also best be described as earthy while, if dry, they have next to no aroma. In either case, "rancid" is an inappropriate term. I think Wasson is building his part up here and selling himself as a hero-adventurer, making colossal sacrifices on our behalf – something which those who followed him weren't shy of doing either, as we'll see.
7. *Life* magazine, June 10, 1957. To read the full article, visit http://www.imaginaria.org/wasson/life.htm Retrieved February 15, 2016.
8. In *Shroom*, ibid.
9. http://mexfiles.net/2010/04/14/maria-sabina/ Retrieved February 19 2016.
10. The "holy children," "sainted ones" or "los ninos" are all names which Sabina gave to her mushrooms.

11. In *Shroom*, ibid.
12. Notably Richard Alpert, later known as the philosopher Ram Dass.
13. See http://www.maps.org/news-letters/v09n4/09410con.html Retrieved February 17 2016.
14. An entheogen is a visionary plant which enables us to reveal and explore "the God within" us.
15. Doblin, R. (1991), 'Pahnke's "Good Friday Experiment": A Long-term Follow-up and Methodological Critique'. *Journal of Transpersonal Psychology* 23 (1): 1–25.
16. Griffiths, R. R.; Richards, W. A.; McCann, U.; Jesse, R. (2006), *Psychopharmacology* 187 (3): 268–83.
17. He finally graduated in 1975 with a degree in ecology.
18. See my book on ayahuasca in this series for more information on this plant teacher.
19. You can read his account of it here: http://realitysandwich.com/168396/experiment_la_chorrera/
20. See the work of James Lovelock for more information on Gaia, the Earth as an aware, self-regulatory system.
21. "Do I have to fuck every woman who comes through here?" he once complained to his roommates at Millbrook. Presumably it was distracting him from his drug-taking.
22. Which he defined, mind you, as five grams of mushrooms taken in a darkened room, so hardly that "heroic" in fact since in my ceremonies everyone gets 5gms, more-or-less, as a matter of course.
23. The most famous incident in fact of something like this happening was when the CIA carried out its MK ULTRA mind control experiments on unknowing human subjects in the 1950s and '60s. On (at least) one occasion a target was given a high dose of LSD without his knowledge or agreement and, unable to handle the effects, he threw himself out of a window to his death. MK ULTRA in *Acid Dreams* by Martin Lee.

24. *Archaeological study explores drug-taking and altered states in prehistory* in Ancient Origins, February 11 2015. http://www.ancient-origins.net/news-history-archaeology/archaeological-study-explores-drug-taking-prehistory-020210 Retrieved November 14 2017.
25. Flesh of the Cods?
26. For more information see my book in this series, *San Pedro: Gateway to Wisdom.*
27. Quotes from *Through the Lands of María Sabina, the search for a shaman in the Mazatec sierra* by Mariel Fatecha. Published in the magazine *Cáñamo de Chile* ,(2012). Also online at http://marielfatecha.blogspot.com.es/2015/05/por-las-tierras-de-maria-sabina-la.html Retrieved November 18 2017.
28. *Through the Lands of María Sabina.* Ibid.
29. *Through the Lands of María Sabina.* Ibid.
30. From *Little Saints,* a documentary examining the use of psilocybin mushrooms in Catholic ritual among the Mazatec people of Oaxaca, Mexico. https://littlesaintsmovie.com/religion_en.html Retrieved November 19 2017.
31. Gordon Wasson, in *Life* magazine 1957. Ibid.
32. In *Shroom,* ibid.
33. Tonāntzin is also referred to as Mother Earth, the Goddess of Sustenance, Honored Grandmother, Bringer of Maize, and Mother of Corn. It is an honorific title comparable to Our Lady or Our Mother. The word *Guadalupe* in this context may derive from *Coatlaxopeuh,* meaning "the one who crushes the serpent," which refers to *Quetzalcoatl* (plumed serpent), the Aztec god of wind and learning.
34. October 15, 2012. http://www.independent.co.uk/life-style/health-and-families/features/magic-mushrooms-and-cancer-my-magical-mystery-cure-8212368.html Retrieved November 24 2017.
35. Online at reset.me. *Psilocybin Mushrooms – Healing From Childhood Trauma and My Spiritual Rebirth.* http://reset.

me/personal-story/psilocybin-mushrooms-healing-from-childhood-trauma-and-my-spiritual-rebirth/ July 30 2015. Retrieved November 24 2017.

36. Read online at https://www.theguardian.com/society/2016/dec/01/magic-mushroom-ingredient-psilocybin-can-lift-depression-studies-show Retrieved November 11 2017.
37. Available online at https://www.vox.com/2016/6/27/11544250/psychedelic-drugs-lsd-psilocybin-effects Retrieved November 29 2017.
38. *Researchers discover that psilocybin mushrooms can cure PTSD, grow brain cells and even erase conditioned fear responses in mice.* July 25 2013. Available online at https://ultraculture.org/blog/2013/07/25/psilocybin-mushrooms-cure-ptsd/ Retrieved November 29 2017.
39. *The Guardian* newspaper, May 29 2017.
40. Read the GDS report at https://www.globaldrugsurvey.com/wp-content/themes/globaldrugsurvey/results/GDS2017_key-findings-report_final.pdf Retrieved November 30 2017.
41. http://www.cdc.gov/features/alcohol-deaths/ Retrieved October 2015.
42. http://www.cdc.gov/tobacco/data_statistics/fact_sheets/health_effects/tobacco_related_mortality/ Retrieved October 2015.
43. http://www.cdc.gov/drugoverdose/ Retrieved October 2015.
44. I have found no scientific studies to show that these assertions are true. In fact, just the opposite; I have included in this book the outcomes of studies which show that psilocybin can *cure* anxiety, panic and depression.
45. For information on books visit https://www.amazon.com/Ross-Heaven/e/B001JP4URE/ref=sr_ntt_srch_lnk_1?qid=1512310824&sr=8-1 and for information on plant medicine diets go to http://www.thefourgates.org/plant-diets/

Moon Books

PAGANISM & SHAMANISM

What is Paganism? A religion, a spirituality, an alternative belief system, nature worship? You can find support for all these definitions (and many more) in dictionaries, encyclopaedias, and text books of religion, but subscribe to any one and the truth will evade you. Above all Paganism is a creative pursuit, an encounter with reality, an exploration of meaning and an expression of the soul. Druids, Heathens, Wiccans and others, all contribute their insights and literary riches to the Pagan tradition. Moon Books invites you to begin or to deepen your own encounter, right here, right now.

If you have enjoyed this book, why not tell other readers by posting a review on your preferred book site. Recent bestsellers from Moon Books are:

Journey to the Dark Goddess
How to Return to Your Soul
Jane Meredith
Discover the powerful secrets of the Dark Goddess and transform your depression, grief and pain into healing and integration.
Paperback: 978-1-84694-677-6 ebook: 978-1-78099-223-5

Shamanic Reiki

Expanded Ways of Working with Universal Life Force Energy

Llyn Roberts, Robert Levy

Shamanism and Reiki are each powerful ways of healing; together, their power multiplies. Shamanic Reiki introduces techniques to help healers and Reiki practitioners tap ancient healing wisdom.

Paperback: 978-1-84694-037-8 ebook: 978-1-84694-650-9

Pagan Portals – The Awen Alone

Walking the Path of the Solitary Druid

Joanna van der Hoeven

An introductory guide for the solitary Druid, The Awen Alone will accompany you as you explore, and seek out your own place within the natural world.

Paperback: 978-1-78279-547-6 ebook: 978-1-78279-546-9

A Kitchen Witch's World of Magical Herbs & Plants

Rachel Patterson

A journey into the magical world of herbs and plants, filled with magical uses, folklore, history and practical magic. By popular writer, blogger and kitchen witch, Tansy Firedragon.

Paperback: 978-1-78279-621-3 ebook: 978-1-78279-620-6

Medicine for the Soul

The Complete Book of Shamanic Healing

Ross Heaven

All you will ever need to know about shamanic healing and how to become your own shaman…

Paperback: 978-1-78099-419-2 ebook: 978-1-78099-420-8

Shaman Pathways – The Druid Shaman

Exploring the Celtic Otherworld

Danu Forest

A practical guide to Celtic shamanism with exercises and techniques as well as traditional lore for exploring the Celtic Otherworld.

Paperback: 978-1-78099-615-8 ebook: 978-1-78099-616-5

Traditional Witchcraft for the Woods and Forests

A Witch's Guide to the Woodland with Guided Meditations and Pathworking

Melusine Draco

A Witch's guide to walking alone in the woods, with guided meditations and pathworking.

Paperback: 978-1-84694-803-9 ebook: 978-1-84694-804-6

Wild Earth, Wild Soul

A Manual for an Ecstatic Culture

Bill Pfeiffer

Imagine a nature-based culture so alive and so connected, spreading like wildfire. This book is the first flame…

Paperback: 978-1-78099-187-0 ebook: 978-1-78099-188-7

Naming the Goddess

Trevor Greenfield

Naming the Goddess is written by over eighty adherents and scholars of Goddess and Goddess Spirituality.

Paperback: 978-1-78279-476-9 ebook: 978-1-78279-475-2

Shapeshifting into Higher Consciousness
Heal and Transform Yourself and Our World with Ancient Shamanic and Modern Methods
Llyn Roberts
Ancient and modern methods that you can use every day to transform yourself and make a positive difference in the world.
Paperback: 978-1-84694-843-5 ebook: 978-1-84694-844-2